FLASHBACK ARTIST

FLASHBACK ARTIST

The remarkable true story of one woman's life and spiritual journey

LISA L. EVERLY

AuthorHouse™
1663 Liberty Drive, Suite 200
Bloomington, IN 47403
www.authorhouse.com
Phone: 1-800-839-8640

First published by AuthorHouse 5/06/2008

ISBN: 978-1-4343-7229-1 (sc)
ISBN: 978-1-4343-7877-4 (hc)

LOC: 2008901658

Printed in the United States of America
Bloomington, Indiana

This book is printed on acid-free paper.

Cover design by Jay Dee Barry & Lisa L. Everly
Inside book design by Jay Dee Barry

authorHOUSE®

To my God and
my mother

ACKNOWLEDGEMENTS

A very special thank you to my partner Jay D. Barry, whose collaboration and design skills brought clarity and structure to my project. To my family and friends…I love you. Thank you for your support and patience during the eight years it took to write this book. I am working on my next book. Please be patient. I promise, it will be worth the wait.

I long for the day when I can simply sit and have nothing else to do, but write.

CONTENTS

And So It Begins...

"Is her mommy going to find her?"

"Yes, she will. She will find you."

I looked away from the angel and back down at my three-year-old body lying virtually lifeless under the large oak tree in our front yard. The grass had grown almost as tall as I was that summer, and I could see my mother frantically searching the dense strands of grass, calling my name as she searched. Her voice seemed to fade away as I looked back toward the angel, who began to sing with me softly.

Finally reaching the tree, my mother knelt down and lifted me from the ground in one sure motion as she turned, calling for my father. The song of the angel faded in my ears and was replaced by my mother's pleas to God for help—I knew he would listen.

I had wandered into the yard after finding my aunt's pills on the coffee table. They looked pretty, like candy, and I had swallowed almost the entire prescription with the exception of a few that fell to the floor, a fortunate indication of what I had done. That many pills were more than enough to carry me into the darkness, and then into the light, where the angel had been waiting for me. I wasn't afraid.

By the time my parents ran to a neighbor's home, borrowed a car and drove me into town to the doctor's office, I had stopped breathing and began turning blue. The doctor said I had escaped death by a few short seconds. After having my stomach pumped and a three-day hospital stay my parents took me home…and that was the beginning of a long journey filled with hope, faith, angels, demons, intrigue, betrayal and always the will to survive in a world that I no longer trusted.

1

Down Time

Tossing and turning all night,
screaming from the inside out, trying to go on with my life,
fighting the anger, hiding the tears, digging deep
...deep within myself just to survive.

I awoke this morning and nearly jumped out of bed, once again feeling angry because I can't seem to fix what's broken.

I let the ice cold water flow over my eyes as I try to erase the traces of tears. I've become very good at starting the day by hiding how I feel, especially when I have to go to work or when I have something important to do that day. "Turning it off" has always been part of my life, and I've become very good at it. By now though, I've been through so much that it's beginning to be hard to hide it, at least from those who have been around me and have gotten to know me. Or rather, have gotten to know me as much as I have allowed them to. Maybe that's the reason I don't get too close to people, keep to myself and fill every moment of my life with activity. I'm trying to avoid those unbearable moments when my mind has the time to focus on what I'm trying so hard not to think about. This is how I've been able to survive.

It may not be the best way, but it is the only way for me—continuing day in and day out to keep up with life's demands while feeling all the time like it would be best to just give up and give in. I not only have to secure my safety, but also work, feed myself, put clothes on my back and survive in this world of people whom I've learned not to trust. Funny, all my life many people have told me that if they were ever to trust anyone with their life, it would be me. I have always wondered who I would someday trust enough to say that to.

Sometimes, well every time, I talk myself right out of giving up by thinking that one day things will get better. I know at this point it can't get any worse and desperately search for the right time to get help and wait long enough to get over another hurdle in my life. But I always feel as though I get past one hurdle only to find that there are more lined up in front of me.

Today as I get started, pull on some clothes and check in the mirror one more time to make sure I look like nothing is bothering me, I sip my tea and think back to when I moved to Oregon. My parents had moved once again, and this time the plan was to run a bait shop/fishing store/BBQ restaurant and campground they'd bought on the banks of the Illinois River in Oklahoma.

I don't remember which move that was for them. I lost track long ago even though Mom kept a precise record of each new house, each new town and each new reason for moving. By the time I was sixteen, my parents had moved 79 times.

I got tired of being the new kid in school and always getting beat up. Finally the day came when Dad told me that the next time someone hits me...kick his ass! That strategy, however, only landed me in the principal's office, where I was swatted with a big wooden paddle by a man who couldn't stand to see a girl kick a boy's ass.

Sometimes when I defended myself I would get kicked out of school because I wouldn't stop until I knew the other kid wasn't going to get up and hit me anymore. I always felt guilty over it, but it was the only way it would stop, and like Dad said, "Once you prove that you won't put up with it, they'll quit doing it." I only wish Mom believed that way, too—maybe she would have put her foot down and Dad would have stopped mistreating her. But no matter what he did to her, she was the one who allowed it.

I eventually became the one who would stick up for the other kids who were being bullied or picked on. I remember walking home from school behind two boys that kept pulling this girl's hair. With her leg brace, there was no way she could get away from them or even turn fast enough to see them sneaking up on her. It broke my heart when one of them punched her in the back, almost sending her to the sidewalk. Chills ran through me when I saw that.

Catching up with them I shoved both boys to the ground and yelled, "Why don't you pick on me? What's the matter with both of you? She's not bothering you." My fists were clenched so tightly that I was digging my fingernails into the palms of my hands. "If I ever see either one of you hitting her again, you'd better get ready for a hell of a fight."

The boys got up and told the girl that they were sorry, and I walked as far as I could with her. By the time we had to go our separate ways I had gotten to know her a little bit. She was a very sweet girl.

Later all four of us became friends and walked home from school together.

But after moving a few more times I just stopped trying to fit in at a new school and opted for spending the day in the park. Oddly enough, Mom never knew I wasn't in school, and I even received passing grades for classes I never attended a moment of.

It was natural for me to stick up for others who were in trouble or couldn't stand up for themselves. I recall when Mom started calling me and informing me of the daily goings on, telling me Dad was treating her badly and that she was afraid of what he might do next, I started to really worry about her safety. I didn't know what to do except listen, be supportive and try to calm her over the phone. But then one day she called and told me that if I was there with her she'd feel so much better and safer—so I hung up and asked my friend Kathy if she wanted to move to Oklahoma with me. She said "Yes," and right away we decided that we would move there to look out for Mom and help run the business.

Before long, we packed up our things and said our goodbyes. The trip from California to Oklahoma was a long one, but I had driven it so many times that I knew every crack in the highway and could drive it without a map.

After a while, I started to notice that everyone on the highway was either pulling over onto the side of the road or lining up under the overpasses. Kathy screamed out, "Oh my God! What is that?" I looked over and saw what made her scream—a tremendous tornado was coming right at us. Debris was flying everywhere and I knew that we would be in a lot of trouble if I stopped and tried to find a safe place at this late date, so I put the pedal to the floor and hoped that we could outrun it.

There was no one on the road at this point, and there was no choice but to just keep going. We must have been moving about a hundred miles an hour as the little U-Haul trailer attached to my truck jumped and shuddered behind us, about to fly off into the storm at any moment. For all I knew the rest of our belongings were being strewn across that Texas highway.

Finally we were out of the path of the tornado and could take a moment to breath. "Wait 'til I tell Mom about this!" I said.

Kathy, still half in shock, sat and looked back at me like she was in disbelief. She didn't say a word as I pulled off onto the next exit so we could stretch our legs and get some air. As we both regained our composure and stopped shaking, I said, "We were lucky."

"That scared the shit out of me. I have never seen a real tornado—much less outrun one," Kathy said.

"Well, you have now."

The trip was long and tiring, but we finally arrived. I was very happy to see my family again, and Kathy was having a good time meeting and visiting with everyone. That night, Mom pulled me aside and told me she was happy I had finally arrived and that she felt so much better with me there.

2

Surviving the Family Business

My mother told me about the conversations she would hear between my dad and his friends and how she was becoming afraid of him. He had even threatened her life. It wasn't long before my dad and his friends began making it very clear that I wasn't wanted there anymore. I had now become the enemy because I was the one helping my mother hold herself together, and I also knew too much about what my dad was involved in, so I was becoming a problem for him and his "upstanding" friends. It was then that I started praying asking God to do something, anything.

I made Mom a promise that I would stay no matter what happened. When it comes to my mother, no one was going to run me off. I will admit that at times I didn't think I could stay another day and that it would have been much easier to just leave, but the fear of what would happen to her without someone there to help always tipped the scales. Dad made several more attempts to talk me into leaving, and his friends continued to make rude comments to me, but I stayed and looked the other way and kept working, even though I was reminded several times how they found others floating down the river without explanation.

I began to feel like I was right in the middle of a dirty little town secret as I watched from a distance the corruption that began to unfold. Watching who came and went, I listened through closed doors, made sure we were safe if we were working late at night in the cafe and even hid a gun for emergencies. I now had the "knowing" realization that Kathy and I had become the enemy.

We became very careful whenever we went anywhere, and we didn't associate with many people. Our reason for being there had changed from helping out with the family business to surviving and protecting ourselves and Mom. Dad was high most of the time and argued with Mom constantly over me and Kathy working in the restaurant. His friends had told him that since we were lesbians it would ruin his business. But, in fact, his friends were the ones ruining the business. Honest, local people sang the praises of Mom's good food and wonderful service.

The cafe and store had become the hang-out for grown men with guns who carried badges to back their vicious egos. Mom and I had a meeting because we could see what was going on and were determined to stop it, one way or another. Dad couldn't understand what was going on because he stayed high on pills and whatever else his pharmacist friend in town brought him, but I watched what the ugly hands of people with power continued to unfold right in front of my eyes. I could see that he had fallen in with a bad crowd that had given him just enough power to keep him wanting more.

I told Kathy that if things got worse and she wanted

to leave, I would completely understand, but I had to stay. When she said she would stay and stand beside me no matter what I was surprised and pleased. But even with that decision made, we eventually decided to get jobs in another town while continuing to be available to help Mom when she needed a break. I felt we made the right decision, because as Mom pointed out, it forced Dad to stay home and help her run the business.

Mom fought Dad every step of the way until he slowed down on the pills. Once that happened he began to realize that his so-called friends were only using him. But, since everyone knew everyone else in that town, and it seemed that if you weren't part of that group you wouldn't make it there, Dad continued to associate with his friends, but much less often. I remember one of his friends telling me, "It's who you know around here." I guess I really pissed him off when I answered back, "That may be true for you, but if you are not part of the solution then you, and those you know, are part of the problem."

The days went by and Kathy and I kept looking over our shoulders. We continued to drive 125 miles round trip to the wheel factory every day for work, which was hard and exhausting. I worked tool crib and Kathy worked the assembly line and before long the stress of work and the ongoing situation with my parents took its toll on me.

We lived on the property behind my parents' business in a one-room, fifteen-foot-by-fifteen-foot A-frame camping cabin that I paid my dad 350 dollars for a month. It had no running water, no toilet and no heat other than a small electric space heater, which I bought. Getting home from the long drive and a hard day's work, we had to walk over to the shower house in the campground if we wanted a shower. There was no hot water, so the shower was cold. With that, combined with everything else, I came down with the flu and had to take off work. Kathy ended up driving to the factory by herself while I was sick.

Not being able to stand the conditions in the A-frame anymore, I went into town with my sister and bought a travel trailer which I parked right behind Mom's house. At least in it we'd have a hot shower and better heat. I moved all of our stuff into it the same day, and when Kathy came home from work that evening, she was ecstatic to find that she now had a warm place to sleep and a hot shower. I heard her cheer out loud in the shower the next morning.

Mom asked me if I would start cleaning the shop and the house, mow the lawn and empty all the trash cans around the campground, so we agreed I'd work in exchange for RV space rent. Kathy wanted to continue working at the wheel factory so we could get back on our feet, save some money and be able to move closer to work when the time came.

We worked very hard, saved our money and continued to help Mom with her business until one particular night when I began to get a hair-raising, everything-turning-gray feeling.

3

Snake-Eyed Bird

Kathy left for work that night as usual, and I did a few things and then headed for bed. A couple of hours later, from a far-off, deep sleep, I heard the familiar noise of what I can only describe as an old-fashioned elevator chime. In the past when I'd been awoken from sleep this way, it meant something was about to happen: I was either going to help someone or witness something. But as usual, I had no idea what would happen or who it might happen to. All I ever knew for sure was that I needed to pay attention and get ready for whatever was coming my way.

I sat up, opened my eyes and said, "What God? What is it?" Of course there wasn't an answer, but I wished there was; it would have made things a lot easier. Earlier, I had felt something coming on, coming closer, but it had been nothing more than a fuzzy gray feeling. I had fallen asleep that night praying because I felt it, and now I was about to find out what it was.

I crawled across the bed and looked out each window, carefully searching the shadows for a clue. I didn't see anything unusual. From my previous experiences, I knew that whatever I was looking for would be easy to recognize, so I pulled on a pair of pants, sweatshirt and jacket and glanced at the clock. It was 1:20 a.m., and there was a lot of the night left. Anything could happen. I went outside and waited.

Closing the door behind me, I turned and looked around. I could see my breath in the cold night air, but still nothing looked out of the ordinary. Ten minutes passed. Suddenly, a feeling came over me, telling me that I needed to look into the night sky. Trees lined the campground in all directions except for one clearing toward the northeast, and that was where I started. As I looked up, I began to hear something, a kind of screech or scream. I closed my eyes and concentrated on the sound. It was almost too far away to hear, but as it got closer the noise became clearer. A chill ran down my spine as the screeching echoed over and over. When I reopened my eyes, I could see what was making the noise.

It was way too dark for me to see with my physical sight, but somehow in my mind's eye, my spiritual eye, the object was clear. At first I thought it was a bird, but there wasn't anything earthly or familiar about it. I would have expected to see it gracefully flapping its wings, or at least an outline of them. As it swooped toward me, the creature looked like it was falling from the sky—and not in an unintentional way. This thing was heading straight for me. I knew this was it—this was why I had been awakened. While this thing may have resembled a bird, I knew that it was something else—something evil.

It came straight at me and though I was fairly certain it intended to hit me, I still hoped that I was wrong.

As a test I decided to stand my ground until the last

moment and then jump out of the way. If it was set on hitting me it would follow; if not, it would miss me and fly into the trailer behind me. Like a batter judging an incoming fast-ball, I took a huge step to the right. Sometimes when things seem a little to weird I will question myself just to be sure things are the way they seem. I stepped to the right at the last minute and It veered too.

With all my focus and intent I yelled out, "God shield me!" but nothing was going to stop its mission, and it hit me hard in the chest. The strike should have sent me flying backward onto the ground, but remarkably, the bird bounced off and landed on the ground right in front of me, shocked and dazed.

It struggled on the ground in front of me, and I could see it was even more unlike any bird I'd ever seen or imagined. Oddly overstuffed, it resembled a cantaloupe and was covered with spikey gray and black tufts that looked more like porcupine quills than feathers. The head was abnormally small and the wings were hardly more than stubs that looked completely useless. Its eyes were unusually large for its tiny head and took up almost half its face. The shape of its eyes reminded me of a snake's, and they had an eerie orange-yellow glow. The beak, which had been open and screeching a moment ago, was wide and hooked at the tip like an eagle or a hawk. This was the weirdest thing I had ever seen in my life!

While it squawked and struggled to get its balance I leaned over it and said, "What's wrong little bird?" Trying not to let on that I was afraid or that I had sensed something unusual about it, I asked, "Are you Okay?" The strange bird centered its feet and then in one smooth motion turned its head completely around and looked me square in the eye. And right then, when I looked into those glowing eyes, I could tell this was not one creature but many. The iris of the eye repeated into itself endlessly like a fun house mirror. Whether they were spirits, demons or some other unnamed beings, there were many of them, definitely evil, and all contained in this one small, overstuffed body.

After staring at me for a moment seemingly in disbelief that it had failed in whatever mission it had tried to accomplish, it started to franticly look in all directions for an escape. Now grounded and vulnerable, it managed to raise itself off the ground and fly a few yards toward the magnolia tree at the back of the trailer.

I knew not to get too close, but I still wasn't sure what this creature had to do with why I'd been awoken by the "elevator chime" and I needed to find out. Following behind it I yelled, "What do you want?" and just as I came upon it again, into my mind came another part of the puzzle, clear and strong. I yelled, "Kathy!" I knew then I had been called to help her, and I also knew the bird was trying to distract me. With this new clarity, I turned and ran as fast as I could toward my parents' house. The creature, gaining strength, or perhaps sensing failure, flew off into the shadows.

Halfway to the house I heard a tremendous crash ahead of me. It sounded like something very large and heavy had smashed into the cliff and sent bits of rock and rubble tumbling down the hill and onto the roadside. A chorus of unearthly cries and screams followed, and the sound, energy and evil entities from inside the creature were loose and rushing in my direction. All I could do was throw myself to the ground and hope the fleeing evil would pass over me. I felt a rush of wind as they flew above me and heard their cries die down. When the leaves finally stopped spinning, I got up and continued running toward the house. I wasn't afraid, but I knew this had been one more delay in getting to where I really needed to be. I had to get to my parents' house, get the truck and find Kathy. I knew she was supposed to be at work until 7 a.m., but something told me she would be there—wherever "there" ended up being.

Rounding the corner of the house, I reached the front door and pounded on it as hard as I could. "Mom! Mom, wake up! I need the keys to the truck!" Finally the door opened and my parents, who were still half asleep, asked what was going on. I didn't have time for a lot of explanation, so I just said, "Give me the keys to the truck! Hurry!" Dad, as usual, couldn't act without reason, but Mom knew that when I needed something it was important. No questions asked, she'd give me whatever I needed and knew I'd explain later. She had finally given up questioning the legitimacy of what I told her long ago, because she always found that it was the truth.

"Hurry, Walt. Get the keys!" she yelled and pointed Dad back into the house. "You be careful, Lisa." Dad came back to the door with the keys, and in a flash I was racing down Highway 17 toward the manufacturing plant where Kathy and I worked. It was over sixty miles away.

Driving as fast as the old truck would go, I flew down the pitch-dark road for what seemed like an eternity. The highway was straight but rolled with small hills and valleys, and the late winter fog hung heavy, keeping me from seeing any further than the next rise. Then finally, I saw my Ford Ranger on the side of the road just up ahead. It sat still and cold on the shoulder of the highway without any sign of life, but also without any sign of foul play. I had found the truck, but had I found Kathy?

Cautiously I drove past the truck, down the road and then turned back. Slowly, I pulled off onto the shoulder a short distance behind, my headlights illuminating the scene. I wondered what I would find in the truck. Was Kathy even there? Had she wandered into the woods or been carried off by someone who had stopped to offer assistance? I was cautious, but then the lights finally came on and I caught the motion of Kathy in the driver's seat. She was here. I thanked God.

I got out of the truck and slowly walked down the center line of the highway. Kathy wasn't rolling down the window or calling out to me, and I wondered why. Was there still something more that would happen tonight? Nearing the truck, I turned and looked into the cab. Kathy finally rolled down the window.

"What happened? Are you all right?" I asked.

I could hear her start to softly cry as she shook her head, "No…How did you find me?"

"God sent me. Are you alone?" I asked.

"Yes," she said so softly I could hardly hear her.

Knowing that I could finally approach the truck, I leaned in through the open window and gently put my arms around her. I felt her relax against my shoulder as she started to tell me how she had ended up on the side of the road.

"I got sick at work," she said, "and had to leave early. I thought I could make it home, but I was so tired that I kept drifting onto the shoulder. I just couldn't go any further. I think I've been sitting here for about twenty minutes, but

I'm not sure..."

I put my hand up to get her to pause for a moment so I could concentrate. "Wait a minute," I said. The feeling was back. I knew this wasn't over yet and that something more was about to happen.

"If anything bad happens, get out of here," I said.

"What's going on?" Kathy asked, sitting up in the driver's seat.

Trying not to frighten her any further, I answered back, "I don't know. It's been a really crazy night. Just roll up the window and stay in the truck."

My tone was stern yet reassuring, and Kathy had been with me long enough to know that when I had "the knowing feeling" it was something to take seriously. She quickly followed my instructions and I prepared myself for whatever might be lurking just outside my sight in the dense fog.

After a moment, I saw a single light appear in the distance from the direction Kathy had just come. The light faded and then reappeared as it moved along the little hills and valleys of the highway. Since it was just one light, I thought it might be a motorcycle, but I listened carefully and couldn't hear the familiar sound. Actually, even as it came closer I can hardly remember hearing any sound at all.

Seconds turned into minutes as I waited for whatever was coming toward me to slowly arrive. When its shape became clearer, I recognized the outline of an old 50s pickup. The single light I had seen was its one remaining headlight. As the beam came to rest on me, I moved out of the center of the road and closer to Kathy, who was half hiding in the cab of the truck, the windows rolled up tightly like I had told her to do.

I remember that the truck seemed camouflaged by its gray primer and rusted and dented patches, which made it blend into the night fog. Trucks like this weren't uncommon since most farmers could keep an old pickup running far past any reasonable expiration, but this truck was different. How its fenders and doors hung onto the chassis was hard to explain, except perhaps that the thick layer of mud somehow held the thing together. The most unnatural thing I remember about the truck though, was the fact that it gave off neither a rattle nor a shimmy, not a clack nor a knock. In fact, its engine ran like it had just come off the line. I had the feeling that this might not be what it appeared to be either. Things just didn't seem to add up.

I again asked God to protect me and Kathy from whatever was coming.

The front windshield was so cracked and smeared with dirt that I couldn't see the driver until the truck pulled up beside me. The look of him startled me. I had seen men like him before. They lived along the river, their camps strewn with old tins of beans and broken bottles of whiskey. His filthy shirt hung around his neck, and his hair fell around his sharp, sunken features in greasy strands.

"Do you…need…any help?" he asked. The words folded out of his mouth with an odd, deep hollowness and a slow, southern drawl.

"No, she's fine now. Thanks," I said.

I looked back at Kathy for a brief moment, and when I turned back to the truck I saw them. The eyes. The glowing snake eyes that had been staring back at me from the creature. For a moment he just sat there, staring at me. I didn't know what was about to happen, but I was ready for anything.

And then, he simply turned his eyes back toward the road and began to laugh. It started out kind of slow, like his speech had been, but then it became louder and faster. The truck started inching forward and his laughter grew stronger. It echoed in my head and clawed at my nerves. As the truck slowly disappeared into the fog, the laughter faded and the silence returned. I let out a long, slow breath of relief and emotional exhaustion. Thank God it was over.

As I turned back toward the truck, Kathy rolled down the window and asked, "What did he say?"

"He asked if we needed any help. That's all," I said and I gave her a little smile of reassurance. She didn't need to know any more than that right now.

"Are you ready to go home?" I asked. "Can you drive?"

"Yes, I think so," she said as she gave me a smile.

I told her to "stay close behind, keep the doors locked and if you can't keep going flash your lights and I'll stop."

Leaning in the window I gave her one more hug and kiss, motioned for her to roll up the window and then walked back to my truck. I pulled forward and waited for her to start the engine and turn on the lights. We slowly drove home and pulled up in front of the trailer. That night I replayed what happened over and over in my head until I fell asleep.

I'm not sure what I prevented that night, but I know it had to do with protecting Kathy and that everything leading up to finding her had been a distraction to keep me from arriving in time. Would she have been murdered by the man in the truck? Or would she have continued driving and veered off the road? I'll never know for sure.

I had been a little worried about how I was going to explain this to Mom, but I did and she understood. I also explained to her that we had decided to move because I couldn't live in such turmoil anymore. She understood that also, but hated to see us go.

Mom left the business a couple of years after we moved away, and my dad...well, he ran off with someone who shared his interest in drugs. It didn't take him long to return to Mom like he'd always done. I no longer blame him for all those times he ran off with someone else. The way I figure it, if a woman will put up with it, then it sends the message that he can continue to treat her that way. I never really understood why she allowed him to do that to her all those years. She was so strong and capable in so many ways.

Kathy moved to Oregon, and I left for the high desert of California.

I was still searching for a safe place where I could try to get over a lifetime of struggle, figure things out and begin healing. Kathy convinced me that Oregon would be a great place for me to live, so I decided to move.

Finding a job had always been easy for me, and I was employed within a week of arriving. Once again I'd be working in security, a field I really enjoyed and was exceptionally good at. My grandfather was once a detective. I was proud to have his genes. My greatest satisfaction was doing my job while treating people with respect and using my brains rather than my brawn. Whether it was patrolling the housing projects of LA or providing security for a movie location, my days in security were some of my happiest and most rewarding.

I began searching for a place of my own because Kathy

already had several people living with her. It was difficult trying to sleep during the day with everyone running in and out so I took showers at Kathy's place whenever it was available and sleep in my truck where I found it peaceful. I worked nights, slept in my truck during the day, and saved up enough money to move into my own space.

Working nights was getting old, but I did it until a day shift became available. After about a year, I was given a raise and a new post at the hospital, but I was once again back on the night shift. It seemed like all I did was work and sleep; I still wasn't getting the opportunity to talk to anyone or begin my healing process, whatever that was going to entail.

Working nights did give me a lot of time to think about my life. I began drawing just to look busy while I relived the pain of my past. I didn't know it then, but it was the beginning of my new life. Art and music began to play a major role in my healing.

CHAPTER 4

A Matter of Respect

There are some days I don't even feel like going to work. But once I'm there the better side of positive thinking comes out and I force myself to make it a better day regardless of how I feel. I have become the master of positive thinking and it's what has kept me alive, along with a few other things I've learned about myself in the last forty some years.

I woke up this morning feeling angry. As tears began to stream down my face, I pulled the blanket over my head and said a quiet prayer. Some days I get tired of having to look in the mirror and convince myself that I can make it through another day.

Before I leave my room I splash cold water on my face to try and wash away the redness in my eyes. I don't like to be asked why I'm crying because there's just too much to tell. Quietly making it out of the house without being confronted is my main objective.

As I sit down at the dining room table to tie my shoes, Terry, my roommate, turns from the sink to say good morning. She stares at me for a moment before speaking.

"How do you do it?"

"Do what?" I ask.

"You know," she says, like she knows I'm trying to avoid the topic, "how do you still continue to go to work, give your all, deal with all those people and their demands, solve problems, and just get through the day feeling like you do?"

Terry has been around me long enough to know when I'm beginning to feel like a ship being tossed against the rocks by the uncertainty of the never-ending, pounding waves. But what Terry doesn't know is what I've already had to endure in my life thus far. My going into detail about how I feel would be a waste of time because I know she couldn't possibly understand.

"I'll be okay once I get to work. It's just that some days are harder for me than others." As I open the front door I call back to her, "See you later."

"Have a good day, Lisa," Terry calls back.

I've always had high standards for being punctual and feel that being early to work shows an employer you have a good work ethic. So punching in fifteen minutes early made me feel like the day was getting better already, and once I relieve the prior officer from his duties the ER show is all mine. I arrange my desk so that I have all the correct tools in front of me to perform my duties. Report forms, notebook, radio, alarm clock, desk bell and pens and pencils are all neatly organized and within reach. I welcome the structure and orderliness of it; it's reassuring.

I learned organizational skills from my mother at a very young age. She told me, "If you know where something lives then you know where to return it. This makes things easier for you when you need it next time because you'll always know where to find it." I enjoy the thought of every-thing having a purpose and a place, like order over chaos.

Every place we ever lived was a home that was organized and clean. Friends and neighbors were always commenting on it and mom would say, "Just because we don't have a lot of money doesn't mean we have to live like pigs."

Sometimes I laugh so hard thinking about all the things my mother would say, but in fact I always paid close atten-tion to what she thought and the way she acted. People who knew her always had positive things to say about her, and I respected that and was very proud of her. Growing up, my mother and my God were the only heroes I had.

As I finish arranging my desk I hear a man yelling at the ER staff and I get up from my chair to evaluate what's going on. There are several people sitting in the waiting room, a couple of guys standing outside the auto-door smoking and a man in his fifties sitting by the phone read-ing a newspaper, all totally disregarding the chaos that is erupting.

I see that the man yelling appears to be alone.

It only takes me a few seconds to evaluate the situa-tion and decide that I can approach him safely. I know my surroundings and have already thought out my plan of action.

The man's voice continues to get louder and more demanding, and as I approach him I take in the details for my report: Caucasian male, five feet nine inches, one hun-dred eighty pounds, greasy dark brown curly hair, dark, heavy and very worn clothes, small black backpack on his shoulder.

Once he sees me coming toward him, he lowers his voice but still mumbles profanities at the nurse and receptionist.

I know how to handle scene makers; they are the ones starved for attention. So I will give it to him.

"Hi! I'm Lisa with hospital security." I hold out my hand to shake his.

"I'm Mr. Johnson," he says as he shakes my hand.

"Is there something I can help you with, sir?"

In a slightly calmer voice, he tells me that his head hurts and all he wants is a couple of aspirin.

I know he isn't going to get anything until he's checked in to see the doctor.

"Mr. Johnson, no one is authorized to prescribe anything to you except a doctor, and in order to see the doctor you must check in with the receptionist first. If anyone gives you medication without a doctor's consent the hospital can be held responsible. We have a policy that any person may see the ER doctor, but they must check in first.

You can always purchase aspirin at your local corner market, or if you prefer, you can check in and see the doctor."

The respect seems to catch him off guard, and he understands what I'm telling him.

"Well, I would like to see the doctor," he says.

As the ER nurse sits down behind the counter, I ask Mr. Johnson to have a seat in the far booth in front of the nurse. "Can I get you something to drink while you wait, Mr. Johnson?" I ask.

"I would love a cup of coffee, if you don't mind."

"I will get you one as long as you're nice to the receptionist. She's the only one we have tonight." He smiles and agrees.

I return with Mr. Johnson's cup of coffee, and he seems

to be getting through the check-in process just fine, with a few minor grumblings here and there.

As I return to my desk, the man who had been sitting next to the phone reading a newspaper moves to the chair by my desk.

"Wow. You were great. I thought that guy was going to punch the receptionist any minute. You must have been doing this kind of work for a long time to have the patience you have."

"Oh, awhile I guess."

"How long have you been working here?" he asks.

"Thirteen or maybe fourteen months," I answer.

"Well, you handled him better than I know I would have. I've been here several times for one reason or another, and all I have to say is they finally found the right woman for the job." He shakes my hand and we both laugh.

"My name is Nick by the way." I introduced myself, too.

Nick continues to read his newspaper while I finish my report. "Hey Lisa, what do you think about what's happening over in Iraq?"

I'm quiet for a moment or two as I take the time to think about Nick's question. I would like to stay in the middle of the road with my answer. "I will tell you that I would hate for a war to break out here in the States. It would be devastating. We do need to keep the terrorists out and protect the American people. Since the beginning of time there has always been war. It's really too bad that a peaceful solution could not have been made over a situation that ends up taking so many lives, but I guess that's what war does.

Nick smiles and folds his newspaper in half. "Not only are you pretty, but you're intelligent, too."

I begin to laugh, which makes Nick laugh.

"Nick? Nick?" the receptionist calls out.

"Oh, that's me," he says as he jumps to his feet. "It was nice talking to you, Lisa. I wish only the best in life for you. We shake hands again, and Nick leaves with the nurse.

I look over and notice that Mr. Johnson is still behaving himself and seems to be waiting patiently, but I can tell he's getting restless.

I check my watch and realize it's time for me to patrol the perimeter and parking lots again. Once I reach the auto-doors I hear Mr. Johnson bark and growl. He then says to the receptionist, "It's just you and me now, baby!"

I turn around and ask him if he would like to go get a breath of fresh air.

"Hell yes. I never thought you'd ask." He jumps to his feet and follows me out.

The receptionist looks up and smiles, followed by a low giggle. She knows once I get him outside I'm going to let him have it…and boy, do I.

Once we get outside, in a much higher octave, yet in complete control, I say, "Mr. Johnson, in case you haven't noticed, you're in the emergency room. You walked in here as if everyone in the waiting room didn't exist. You were evaluated on your illness or emergency, and even though you didn't see it, there is a patient in the back, probably in surgery by now, within minutes of his life. The ER staff here knows by their years of experience which patients are in more of a life-and-death situation. You came in here yelling and demanding aspirin for your headache. My question to you, Mr. Johnson, is do you realize how disruptive you have been, not to mention disrespectful to the other patients, ER staff and myself? And, believe it or not, you are showing everyone that you don't even have respect for yourself. I went as far as to get you a cup of coffee. I am not saying your emergency is not important, but rather, I'm saying have some respect. This is where people come to get help!"

He's now staring at the ground like a scolded schoolboy. Softly he says, "I have always wanted to be a doctor."

This completely throws me. It's not what I am expecting from him as he looks up at the neon emergency entrance sign and says, "It's time I get my shit together." Smiling, he apologizes and asks for a hug.

I hesitate at first, but I'm sure it is in good faith at this point.

The nurse finds us outside and requests his presence. "The doctor is ready to see you now."

I think there's a reason for everything, and my encounter with Mr. Johnson is another reason to believe.

Star Warrior

© Lisa L. Everly 2006

Cloud Dancer

© Lisa L. Everly 2006

5

Rebuilding a Dream

As I sit down I say a little prayer for Mr. Johnson and ask God to help him put his life back together and perhaps even find a way to work on rebuilding his dream of being a doctor. Maybe our conversation will be the catalyst that changes everything. We never know what small thing may create a large change in our overall perspective.

Now that things have settled down a bit I take note of what's going on in the ER. Things are pretty much the same as before Mr. Johnson arrived. I see a father and son; the boy looks to be about thirteen and the dad is keeping him occupied by pointing out articles in a Road and Track magazine they're reading.

I overhear him say, "I had one just like that when I was in college. Darn thing was a piece of junk when I bought it, but I worked all summer on it and got it going." Then looking over at his son, he adds, "How about when you get feeling better, we pick up a project car? I bet if we work on it every weekend we'd have it running by the time you get your permit."

The boy smiles and nods his head in agreement just as

the nurse comes to get them. The dad asks if he can take the magazine with them, and the nurse says yes.

I used to work on cars with my dad, too. He is an excellent mechanic, and looking back I could have really used his advice on my dream truck, which quickly turned into my mechanical rite of passage.

Straightening the paper and pens on my desk once again, I remember how it all went and smile as I recall what small thing triggered one of my changes in perspective. Sometimes there's nothing as powerful as being told you can't do something.

When I was about seventeen, I saved my money and bought a '65 Chevy truck from a car lot for 800 dollars. As I drove off the lot I was smiling ear to ear, but by the time I got on the highway I was fuming mad because the truck began to smoke like a freight train. The engine began knocking so loudly that I couldn't hear the Pioneer Super Tuner stereo surrounded by six speakers, which was one of the main reasons I'd bought the truck.

Having spent all the money I had to buy the truck of my dreams, I then had to figure out how I was going to fix it. One way or another, I was going to be driving that truck back to California.

All week long I caught a ride to work because I didn't trust that my truck could make the twenty-mile drive, but when payday came I crossed my fingers and drove into town to see how much a mechanic would charge to fix it. The quote to overhaul the engine was between 600 and 800 dollars, but he may as well have said 8,000. I told him I didn't have that kind of money, and he suggested I buy a kit at the auto parts store and do it myself. I stood there considering my options for a moment until he walked off laughing. After that, there was but one option. I climbed in my truck and drove straight to the auto parts store.

Scraping together every cent I had, I bought the kit and a how-to book. Between the hours I spent working on engines with my dad and reading the instruction manual, I was pretty confident it wouldn't take me more than a day or two. Now all I needed were a few tools.

I stopped off at my friend Tim's house to borrow the tools I thought I'd need, but in the end I was still missing one important piece—the cherry picker. I hoped that a strong limb and a length of chain would suffice as an adequate replacement. Other than that, I thought I had everything, until Tim handed me a very large hammer.

"This is for just in case everything else fails," he said with a big grin on his face. "Just in case my mission fails and I'm in imminent danger of a complete meltdown. Right sir?" I said as I tried to look completely serious. We both broke into peals of laughter as I gathered up the box of tools and left.

Heading back down the road, the knocking and sputtering were getting worse. I kept my fingers crossed that it would make it to where I needed to go. I knew it was on its last leg, and I certainly didn't feel like pushing it the last mile to my friend's mother's house.

When I pulled up at Gail's house and asked if I could borrow her yard for a few days, she laughed. I told her what I needed it for and she stared at me for a moment and then asked if I knew how to fix a riding lawn mower. "Not a problem," I told her. "That's a fair trade." I decided to fix her lawn mower first, to eliminate the risk of losing any stray parts in the tall grass.

As I parked my truck under the big oak tree, Gail was

happily mowing her yard and waving to me. Waving back, I unloaded the chain and set out the tools side by side in two perfect rows along a tarp. I set the instruction manual down alongside the tools and decided I had everything I needed, I just wasn't sure where to start. I'd watched my dad work on his truck several times, and I recalled that he always took the hood off first. So that's where I started.

It was heavy and awkward, but I managed to lift it off the truck and onto the ground without too much trouble. Once I tore into the engine though, that was a different story. After about an hour, I began throwing tools, rocks and everything else I could find. By the end of the afternoon, the hammer Tim gave me came in handy, too.

I sat down and cried. Nothing seemed to be going right so I decided to call it a day and began walking home. It was hot and every step I took down that dirt road was just one more step away from my dream truck.

About halfway home, I reached a "Y" in the road and heard loud music coming from a lone dust cloud just out of sight in the opposite direction. It was the group Boston and the song was "Don't Look Back." I began to laugh because that was exactly what I was thinking at the moment: "Should I keep going or do I go back?"

I must have thought about that question for a while as I walked, because the next thing I knew I was standing in my driveway. The car with the blaring stereo was right in front of me, slamming on its breaks and sending dirt and dust in all directions. When I was finally able to see through the debris, I realized it was Rhonda, one of my mother's friends. She was grinding the gears, trying to put the car into reverse. I decided the porch was a safer place to wait for her.

Finally bringing the car to a stop, she jumped out and began running toward me. It frightened me to see that she was covered in blood and her face was swollen with large patches of black, blue and purple. Almost stumbling and falling to her knees, she reached out to me and caught herself.

"He tried to kill me, Lisa!" she said, half sobbing and half screaming. "And this time the bastard did it in front of the kids!"

I don't think she knew whether to be furious or scared to death, whether to run away or go back. All I could do was take her by the arm and get her to sit down on the porch to catch her breath.

"Where are the kids now? Are they all right?" I asked.

"I just dropped them off at my mom's," she said as she wiped blood from her lip. "What am I going to do, Lisa?"

I could tell that her heart was broken more than anything else. She was cut, bruised and bleeding physically, but emotionally her hopes and dreams for her family and children had finally been shattered beyond repair. This time, all his promises and all her denial couldn't put it back together again, and that was what hurt the most. This time, her soul was cut too deep.

She told me how she had made a run for it when he had gone into the bathroom and how she would never forget the feeling of knowing she could be killed if he caught her trying to escape.

"Come on inside, Rhonda. I'll get you some ice for that bruise." I gently took her hand, helping her to her feet.

Once inside, I found Rhonda a seat at the dining room table and got her a glass of water and a kitchen towel filled with ice cubes.

"I knew I'd be safe here," she said, holding my hand for a moment as she took the towel.

And then suddenly, with a smile and a laugh, she said, "I didn't even know how to drive his car until I jumped in and took off."

"I never would have guessed that, Rhonda," I said, trying not to smile.

We both paused for a moment and then broke out in a round of laughter, remembering the scene that had just taken place in the driveway. It was a welcome relief, but soon her eyes were filling with tears again as she said, "My poor kids. They were scared to death."

I reminded her that this wasn't the first time it had happened and asked if she was going to do something about it. Enough was enough.

"I can't support three kids by myself," she said, "and I talked to the preacher and he keeps telling me that I just need to be patient and pray. He's just having a hard time because things are difficult at work right now."

"What does the preacher know about your life? Be patient for what? The next time he decides to take things out on you and the kids? By then it will be too late and you could end up dead…then who'll be taking care of your three kids? And, since when does God say it's okay to beat the livin' daylight out of someone just because you've had a hard day?" I found myself starting to yell and clenching my fists. I wanted to get through to her, but she didn't need me angry as well, so I sat down beside her and tried to calm down. Holding her hand, I took a deep breath and talked to her very directly.

"Go to the police and file a report, and if you have to, stay at your mother's until you can get on your feet. Get a few friends and family members together and make sure you have a police officer there when you move out. Pack your things and never look back." Then I squeezed her hand a bit more and looked right into her eyes when I said, "You're going to be okay. You can do this." She gave a little smile and nodded her head.

Helping her to the couch, I asked if she wanted me to take her to the hospital. She shook her head 'no,' so I told her to rest and take as much time as she needed. I was filthy from my day's struggle with the engine block and needed to shower. When I came back in the room, she was on the phone with her mother, telling her that she was going to the hospital and together they were making plans for herself and her kids.

"Thanks, Mom. I love you, too," Rhonda said as she hung up the phone and sat back on the couch. A weight had been lifted from her, and the fear had been replaced with determination. I guess you could say she was "driving her own car" now and not just sitting in the passenger seat while someone else drove it over a cliff. There is tremendous power in taking control of your own direction instead of handing that power to others.

Composed, she said she was ready to head off to the hospital to get checked out. I walked her to the porch and gave her a long hug and reassured her again that everything would work out.

"Thanks, Lisa," she said. "When are you leaving for California?"

"As soon as possible. I hope this week. I'm having a bit of a truck problem."

"I'm going to miss you. I have never known anyone like you in my life," Rhonda said as she threw her arms around me again. "You're always helping everyone else, and every time I see you, you're doing everything by yourself."

I smiled and hugged her back. There was nothing I could say about her observation—that's just the way it had always been. Which reminded me, I still had a truck to fix or else I'd never be getting to California.

Rhonda made her way down the stairs and back into the driver's seat. With a turn of the key, the engine came to life and she smoothly shifted into drive. Leaning into the car window, I once more wrapped my arms around her and repeated a few words of encouragement. Then I saw the solution to my truck problems sitting on the back seat.

"Hey, Rhonda, what are you going to do with that roll of masking tape in the back?"

"It belongs to dip shit. Why? You need it?" she said as she reached around behind her and tossed the roll to me.

"Thanks. You just made my day."

"You made my day, too. Believe me. I really feel better now," she said with a big smile as she headed down the driveway and disappeared in a musical cloud of dust. This time it was Journey.

The next morning when I awoke it was pouring down rain, but I was determined to get the engine torn apart before dark. Soaked to the bone, I scraped my knuckles, yelled and threw tools everywhere as I worked like a woman possessed. But this time, whenever I took something out I wrapped it with the masking tape and numbered it. Nothing was going to be unaccounted for if I could help it.

With all the secondary parts disconnected and the motor mounts unbolted, it was time to try lifting the engine out of the truck. After a couple of tries, I managed to swing a chain over the lowest, strongest branch of the tree. While bracing my back against the trunk of the tree and my foot against the front bumper, I pulled as hard as I could. Somehow, I managed to lift the engine up just enough to push the truck away with my feet and then lower the engine to the ground. Now all that was left was to take off the head and strip down the block.

With only minutes before sundown, I had taken the entire engine apart and cleaned all the pieces with gasoline. In the process, I'd discovered where the loud noise was coming from. With a little over an hour before the auto parts store closed, I decided to head into town.

Fortunately, I caught a ride with a man who owned a dairy down the road. He picked me up on the side of the highway. Even though I was soaking wet, he insisted on giving me a ride into town.

"I see you're busy working on your truck," Mr. Trenton said.

"Yeah, it's a lot of work."

"Don't you have a husband or father or a brother to help you do that?" he asked.

"My family is in California, and I'm not married."

"Well, I just don't think you're going to be able to do it all by yourself. I mean, have you ever rebuilt an engine before? I wouldn't attempt it, even though I work on my farm equipment now and then. I'm not a mechanic," he said.

Without wanting to seem rude I replied, "I'm sure I'll figure it out. I mean, I don't see any volunteers."

Laughing, he changed the subject and began talking about how the price of pesticides was going up and he didn't know how he was going to spray his fields next year. I politely listened all the way into town and then thanked him when I got out at the parts store. "I guess everyone has something they worry about," I thought to myself.

I woke up the next morning knowing I was going to drive my truck that day, and nothing was going to stop me. As I walked down the road toward it, my confidence grew with every step, and I visualized how each piece would fall back into place smoothly. Then I came close enough to see it parked under that big oak tree.

With the hood off and miscellaneous parts piled about, it looked like every other truck that is set out behind a house with every intention of repair, only to be left indefinitely, eventually taken over by the tall grass, rust and the occasional raccoon searching for a warm winter home. But that wasn't going to be my truck's fate. We were leaving for California tomorrow.

Not fifteen minutes later, there I was yelling at the top of my voice. I kicked every tire twice and then tore off the rearview mirror and threw it as far as I could into the woods. Sitting down in total frustration, my earlier confidence seemed like a cruel hoax.

Once I calmed down, I got right back up and went to work. Another day and there I was at sunset, walking home down that long dirt road. But at least one thing was for sure: I'd finally get to drive my truck home…tomorrow.

"Tomorrow" came and went, and once again I found myself walking home instead of driving. I told myself I was going to push back my departure just one more day. And then another "tomorrow" came, and I saw the sun go down as I walked home.

After a total of four days, I finally found myself standing in front of the truck. I was ready to connect the battery cables. It was finally done, and with tremendous relief I tightened each side down, climbed in the driver's seat and put the key in the ignition. Closing my eyes, I took a deep breath, quietly said "Please, God. Let it start," and turned the key. I only heard a clicking sound, but that was enough. I knew it would probably fire up with a jump start.

Since my uncle lived nearby I called and asked if he could come over with his cables. He said he'd be right over, and I sat down under the tree and tried to wait patiently. With success just within reach, the minutes seemed to turn into hours.

When he arrived, we hooked the truck up and let it charge for about ten minutes. Gail came over to say hello and see how we were doing.

"Gail, this is my uncle Will. He's a preacher," I said.

"Nice to meet you, preacher," Gail replied as she shook his hand. "Lisa's been giving us quite a show out here these last few days."

"I can't believe she did this all by herself," he said, patting me on the back with a big grin.

"She sure did and it was quite comical, too!" Gail added. "I saw her throw rocks, sticks and even kick the tires, but I lost it this morning when Tommy yelled at me to come to the window. I looked out and saw Lisa throwing everything inside the truck out the cab window. Then I saw her pull off the rearview mirror and throw it as hard as she could into the woods. It's probably still out there!"

My uncle started busting stitches and tried to catch his breath as his face turned bright red. He asked what I was going to do now that I didn't have a rearview mirror, and I said that I hardly ever used it so I doubted it would make any difference. Uncle Will realized I wasn't finding the play-by-play as funny as he did, so he changed the topic.

"When are you going to California, Lisa?"

"Tomorrow."

"Tomorrow? Don't you think you should wait a couple of days to see if the truck will make it? With a new engine you'll want to test it out for a day or so, won't you?"

"Oh, it will make it one way or another. If not, I'll leave it next to the Cadillac Ranch with all fours up."

Uncle Will belted out a laugh that scared me to death. I thought he was going to get the Holy Ghost right then and there.

"You are so funny, Lisa! God loves you so much," he chuckled. "If you would just stay a couple more days you could go to church with us on Sunday."

"Now Uncle Will, I of all people know God loves me, and it doesn't take me sitting in church to prove I love him, too," I said politely but still making my point.

"Well, I'm going to pray that I see you at church on Sunday," he continued.

"And I'm going to pray that I not only make it safely to California, but that I beat my dad's all-time record of twenty-four-and-a-half hours with my new rebuilt engine!" I said with confidence as I started and stopped the engine several times to make sure the battery had charged long enough.

Seeing that he wasn't going to win this one, Uncle Will offered to help me put the hood back into place. While I tightened the bolts, he held it steady. Soon, I was standing in front of my dream truck once again.

"Nice…" I whispered to myself as I wiped a greasy fingerprint from the grill. "Thanks for coming, Uncle." I said as I gave him a big hug.

"Well, drive safe and tell your mom and dad I said hello."

As Uncle Will drove away I heard Gail calling me for dinner. Real southern food—as comforting for the soul as it is for the stomach. Homemade relish, sweet butter, cheese corn bread, fried okra, hominy, pinto beans and ham, fried green tomatoes and corn on the cob, with sweet tea to wash it down. It was the perfect ending to a perfect day. Afterwards, I stayed and helped Gail clean up and said my goodbyes.

When I walked back to the truck I climbed in the cab and turned the key. It started up on the first try! I was grinning from ear to ear as I turned up the Pioneer Super Tuner. After I returned all the tools I'd borrowed I stopped off at the store, and there in the parking lot was the mechanic who had laughed when he suggested I fix it myself.

"Wow. Looks great!" he said as I lifted the hood for him to take a look. "Who'd you have do it?"

"It took me four days," I said, closing the hood.

"Want a job?"

"No. I'm on my way to California."

As I recall I did break my dad's record, and the truck ran great all the way there. I still have a tremendous feeling of satisfaction in having done that all by myself. The only thing that was missing was the rearview mirror. I never did find the darn thing.

Getting up from my desk now, I walk over and rearrange the magazines in the waiting room and make a mental note that I need to replace the issue of Road and Track. The table seems incomplete without it.

6

My Arrival

Returning to my station, I pull out a piece of paper and a couple of my favorite ball points. I draw a line straight down the center and then another in a long 's' curve overlapping it. "Good start," I think to myself, "but what is it?" I'm not getting a feel for it tonight. Maybe I'm trying too hard.

Just as I'm about to crumple up the sheet and throw it in the trash under my desk, I notice an older sedan pulling up to the ER door. It's coming in pretty fast, and as it jolts to a halt, its shocks still bouncing, a tall, young man jumps out and runs around to the passenger door.

I start preparing for whatever situation might be coming. With the young man as frantic as he is, I figure it might be something drastic, so I quickly look to see where the nearest wheelchair is and if there's a nurse available. One of them has noticed as well and is moving in the direction of the man—who's now trying to gently, yet quickly, move a very pregnant girl from the car.

With one hand he is holding her up long enough for the nurse to get the wheelchair into place, and with the other he's trying to carry an overnight bag and dial a cell phone, which ends up balanced under his chin. As he reaches down to pick up the fluffy pink baby booties that have fallen from the overstuffed bag, I wonder if I should follow behind him to pick up the pieces.

The girl, who doesn't look much older than nineteen, is taking it all in stride while looking a bit embarrassed that he is making such a fuss. She seems calm and happy as he wheels her past my desk.

"It's going to be fine honey. Just calm down," she says to him. "Did you get ahold of mom and dad yet?"

"Just keep breathing, baby!" he says as if he didn't hear a word. "Remember, in through your nose, out through your mouth! Are you in pain? Do you want a drink of water? How close are the contractions?"

I think to myself, "If this guy doesn't slow down and take a deep breath I'll be needing a wheelchair for *him*."

Seeing the two of them brings back so many memories of how hard I had tried to have a baby but couldn't and the stories my mom told me about how I came into this world. It's nice to see how safe the girl feels and that she has family with her and more on the way. That is very different from how things were when I was born.

I remember the story as if I'd been right there with her. Well, I suppose I was.

I can clearly see my mother, Mary, being wheeled into the small city hospital in Tahlequah, Oklahoma, in 1963.

Klink, klank, klink. The wheelchair rolled down the hall toward the maternity ward. The nurse pushing the chair didn't say a word to the frightened sixteen-year-old who's clutching a small carpet bag in her lap as she searches every passing face for a friendly smile and a bit of comfort.

She was also searching for an explanation of what was happening to her. No one had told her about labor and contractions or how much pain there would be. She figured that somehow she'd just know things once she was married and that there was some magical knowledge that would develop once she had "grown up." Or perhaps, it was something her husband was supposed to tell her, just like how to be with him in the dark or how to make his favorite food. But no matter how the information was supposed to come to her, it never arrived, and now here she was trying to figure it all out for herself.

Earlier she'd been brought to the hospital by her father-in-law, Grover Everly. Her husband, who was only seventeen himself, was in Kansas for the wheat harvest. There was no one else to help except for her father, "Paper Sack" Kelly, and she wasn't sure if he'd come to the hospital or not. The chair came to a halt at a darkened room, and the nurse helped Mary into a bed and shut the door behind her.

Labor went on for thirteen hours when finally a nurse came in and told her it was time to go. "Go where?" she asked, but no one answered. Soon she was rolling back down the corridor and into a different kind of room with bright lights and a sterile metal table. A doctor in a stiff white jacket was chatting with a pretty, young nurse. No one said a word as the nurse who was pushing the wheelchair helped Mary onto the table.

Finally aware that there was a patient to attend to, the doctor stopped his banter and took a quick look at the job ahead. He gave a few brief instructions to the nurse who then disappeared into the dispensary.

Moments later, hands were holding her down as a mask was placed over her face. A distinctive smell started to seep in and Mary panicked and tried to hold her breath, but it was no use. As the nurse moved closer the gas began to take over and she started to fade into twilight. With one last flutter of her eyes, she saw the doctor coming closer and his fingers disappearing beneath the nurse's starched white skirt. Then there was darkness.

Distracted, the nurse administered too much ether and before long Mary was floating through a long, dark tunnel to the other side. Once through, the darkness was replaced by a bright white light and the soft sounds of water flowing over stones. There was such peace on the other side, and so many answers! Not just the answers about what was happening to her at that moment, but all the answers to every question she had ever asked. The answers to her questions about the Universe, God and why we exist were alive, and everything was so clear.

Along with that knowledge came a message about the daughter she was giving birth to. The message was about the importance of her life, the role she'd play in the realm of Spirit and a name: FéLisa LáVonne. Not a usual name for a baby girl born in a small town in Oklahoma.

Then, from far off in the back of her mind, Mary herd her daughter's cries. It was not her time to stay in the light, so she traveled back through the tunnel where she found herself, once again, alone and frightened in a dark hospital room. Her baby was nowhere to be found. But even more frightening was the realization that the knowing was gone. All the answers had disappeared. Mary struggled to grasp and reconstruct the pieces of the message with only the vaguest memory. But it was no use. Blackness came again and it was gone.

Happy voices from the woman in the next room greeted Mary as she finally awoke. She was still alone, and all she could do was lay there and listen to another mother laughing with her family, oohing and aahing over baby presents they'd brought her. Mary wondered if anyone would come to see her.

"Why is the room still dark, and why haven't I seen my baby yet?" Mary thought to herself. "Where is my baby? Is she all right?"

Starting to panic, Mary tried to get out of bed just as a nurse entered the room. Laying her down again, the nurse said, "Now, now. You have to stay in bed."

"My baby! Where is she?" Mary screamed as she began to cry, wondering why no one was listening to her.

For three days this went on, until the door finally opened and there was a nurse holding the tiniest little bundle she'd ever seen. Taking the child into her arms, she hesitated and then pulled the blanket away from her face.

"Oh, my heavens. There you are!" she said in a low voice just as the baby's eyes fluttered open to look at her. "Just wait until your daddy sees you."

"Mary, is this the first time you've seen your baby girl?" the nurse asked.

"Yes, it is," she said, not taking her eyes off the baby for even a moment.

Then the nurse asked hesitantly, "Mary are you married?"

"Yes. My husband is in Kansas on the wheat harvest. The man who brought me to the hospital is my father-in-law."

Suddenly, the nurse rushed out of the room. Mary looked down at her daughter and whispered "Fe'Lisa La'Vonne is your name. What big, beautiful brown eyes you have, just like your daddy's."

More voices filled with laughter floated in from the corridor, but this time it didn't seem to matter because she had the most beautiful little baby staring back at her. "Thank you, God," she whispered. As she looked up, her father was standing by her bed, smiling from ear to ear. He was dressed in his Sunday best and wearing a brand new paper sack rolled up and sitting properly on the top of his head. Reaching down, he gently took the baby from Mary's arms.

"That's the sweetest little thing I've ever seen, Mary."

Another knock came at the door and after a brief pause a nice looking gentleman wearing a suit entered the room. "What a beautiful baby girl she is," said the well-spoken man. "This is for her." He handed Mary a small book called *Hope of a Nation,* which was filled with bible stories. She thanked him. "Make sure you read that to her," he said as he slowly closed the door behind him.

Papa Kelly gave a little laugh and said to the baby, "look at that, little Lisa. Your first gift is a book from a Methodist preacher. So, I guess this will be your next present." He reached into his jacket and took out a little paper sack, the size kids filled with penny candy. Carefully rolling the sides down perfectly he folded the crease flat and set the tiny hat on the small table beside Mary's bed. Then, reaching into his pocket again, he presented a shiny, new silver dollar. "This is yours too, little Lisa." He set the coin on the baby's blanket and bent down to kiss her forehead. "She is very special, Mary. God loves her."

Collecting his coat, Papa Kelly gave Mary a warm smile and said he had to get back to Mary's six other brothers and sisters, who were at home waiting to hear the good news.

Mary realized she hadn't unwrapped the baby except for her head and recalled something about having to count fingers and toes. Cautiously, she unfolded the blanket and counted…she had ten of the cutest little fingers and toes, all absolutely perfect. Mary let out a sigh of relief and smiled.

Later, a nurse came in with a plate of food and told Mary she'd be going home in the morning. Now they were being nice to her, but for the last five days she'd been lonely, scared and pushed aside by staff who thought she was just another unwed mother giving birth to an illegitimate child.

The next day, Grover came to pick Mary up from the hospital. Along with the baby, the hospital handed her six diapers, two receiving blankets, twelve safety pins and two T-shirts—the only baby items she had. Grover helped Mary into the car and set the baby in a Clorox box on the floorboard for the ride home.

When they arrived at Grover's shack in the woods, along the banks of the Illinois River, he gently moved little Lisa out of the box and into a dresser drawer lined with a few of his shirts. There was no running water and no bathroom, but it was clean and safe. Grover helped Mary by picking up the dirty diapers every day, washing them by hand and hanging them on the tree branches to dry. With Grover helping, Mary was able to spend more time bonding with her new baby, making up for the time a the hospital.

A few months later, Lisa's dad come home from the wheat harvest, and they were finally a family. Together, they moved into a little house on a long dirt road just outside town. My sister was born a year later, and then my brother a year after that when we'd moved to Texas. I don't know how my mother did it—three kids in three years.

"Excuse me. Can you tell me where room 312 is?" a voice says.

Startled back into the present, I reply, "What? Oh, yes…

sorry. Take the elevator to the third floor, 312 to the right.

I smile and pull myself back together so I can begin my rounds.

Thinking back, I recall something else Mom told me. When I was almost a year old, my dad's father, grandpa Everly, came to the house, picked me up and with tears in his eyes said, "It would have been better if you had never been born." Then he drove himself to the hospital and died minutes later of a heart attack. I wonder what he meant by that and why it was one of the last things on his mind.

I feel that quite a bit of good has come from my life, but maybe he had a premonition about how difficult and dangerous my life was going to be. Considering everything that happened to me during my first three years, I can understand why he would have said that. My uncle missed shooting me in the head by just a couple of inches, I overdosed on my aunt's tranquilizers and almost died, and my grandfather Kelly accidentally ran over my legs with his car. Poor grandpa, he was so shaken by everyone yelling that he put it in reverse and ran over me again.

I look down at my desk and see a pen still in my hand, poised over the paper. Apparently, my hand took on a life of its own while I was thinking, and I'd drawn a swirling bouquet of flowers and leaves. Brightly colored blossoms of high lighter orange and Pilot roller ball black open in all directions, looking more like mouths than flowers, while long, thin leaves of green weave through them.

"Hey, good one!" my co-worker Jen says as she passes my desk. "How do you keep coming up with this stuff? I can't even draw a straight line."

I thank her and make a mental note that I should send this one to Mom.

7   Shoelace Solution

I begin my rounds and as I turn the corner I notice an intoxicated man wobbling and cursing at the top of his voice, standing in the middle of the street with only seconds before an oncoming car will enter the intersection.

Grabbing my flashlight from my duty belt, I run toward the intersection and get the driver's attention just as the man falls to the pavement. The oncoming car sees me and slows down just in time to swerve into the other lane, barely missing the man lying in the middle of the street.

I get him to the curb by convincing him that his shoelaces need tying. Once he sits down, I tie his laces together in a tight knot that can't easily be undone. As he rolls around on the ground vomiting and cursing, I call the local police department and stay with him until they arrive. It was a close call for him, and he won't even remember it tomorrow.

The excitement has attracted a few bystanders and a couple of patients who had been waiting in the emergency room. They are laughing hysterically, partly because I had thought to tie his laces together and partly because of his reaction to discovering that his feet no longer worked like he expected. One woman leans over to me and says, "That was a great idea! I'm going to try that on my husband."

"It doesn't take much to save a life," I say.

To some it may seem like a silly solution, but I just want to make sure the guy doesn't hurt himself, me or someone else.

I return to my desk to write up the report. As I sit down, Trish, the ER nurse, approaches me. "Hey, Lisa. Whatever it was you said to Mr. Johnson earlier must have turned his heart line or something. He became the sweet-est man. I mean, it was like Dr. Jekyll and Mr. Hyde!" I have to laugh, remembering what he'd said earlier about wanting to be a doctor.

"Before Mr. Johnson left, he told the doctor that he would never forget his experience here and what the security lady told him. So, what did you tell him? We're all curious."

"Nothing that he didn't already know."

"Well, the ER staff, as well as myself, want to thank you for what you do around here. We love the way you handle things. In case you didn't know, you are making a big dif-ference in a lot of people's lives. Thank you, Lisa, for all your hard work."

"Thanks, Trish. That's my job."

"No, I think it's your life, and you're good at it," she says.

There is always someone to help, and even though at times it has nothing to do with the hospital or my job, I'm not the type of person to look the other way when I see someone in danger. It is in my human nature to do the right thing—even though a lot of the time people haven't done right by me. I get a lot of happiness and satisfaction from helping others.

The ER is now empty. I won't say the "quiet" word, because an orderly once told me that as soon as I do, all hell will break loose—so I don't tempt fate.

It's about 2:30 a.m., and I pull out a piece of plain white paper from my bag and begin to doodle. I decide to sit at my desk during my break since I forgot to bring anything to eat. One of the girls from the ER staff is on her way to get a soda and asks me if I'd like something. I quickly cover my drawing with my hand. "No, thank you," I answer.

She puts her hand on top of mine and asks, "Can I see what you're drawing?"

I slowly move my hand away, revealing another piece of my life.

"Wow! Pretty good for just passing the time. That's the most beautiful flower I have ever seen anyone draw."

"Thanks. Drawing helps me think," I respond. "Have a nice break."

"Thank you." Her voice echoes from down the hall.

I'm beginning to make sense of what it is I'm sketching. I don't consciously look at the paper while I'm drawing—each sketch materializes on its own, yet they reveal remarkable detail and clarity. Funny thing is, I never even knew I could draw.

As I continue, I begin to visualize myself and hear the screams that never left my clenched teeth. I'm six years old, lying in bed and scared to death that the squares on the ceiling are going to kill me.

My pen is hard at work with no indication of stopping anytime soon. I think back remembering how I'd counted the squares on the ceiling over and over again while I was being raped.

I remember my mom and dad leaving me and my younger brother and sister with their best friends, Flora and Pete, while they went to visit grandpa, who was extremely ill. Flora and Pete were very good to us, as was their daughter Lena, but their other daughter Ruth, who was in high school, was horrible and would do the most terrible things to us until Lena would discover what she was doing and come to our rescue. I begged to go with mom and dad to see grandpa, but it was decided that my brother and sister and I were too young for the trip and that it would be traumatic.

My mother is the oldest of seven children and her father was a very interesting man. People called him "Paper Sack" Kelly because he wore a paper sack on his bald head. Mom said it was to keep the sun from burning his head while he painted signs and billboards out in the scalding sun. I can still remember him giving us kids chocolate malted milk tablets, which he said were full of vitamins that would make us big and strong. He told me once that his favorite thing in life was to be with his three grandchildren, telling us stories of his life. I loved my grandpa, and to this day he is the finest man I have ever known. I still remember every detail of the stories he told us.

Grandpa worked for the same security company I'm working for now. Probably the most valuable thing he taught me was to treat people with respect while securing the safety and possessions of others. "You'll get respect if you give it," he'd say.

Besides working in security, grandpa excelled in a number of other occupations. In Chicago he was a tap dancer and during the early thirties he hosted his own radio show over the San Antonio Airway. He also worked with champion boxers and ran a circus where he interviewed Lucille Ball for a song-and-dance position but suggested she go into comedy instead.

He seldom received the recognition he deserved and few people knew that he was the original inventor of the neon sign and built the first home on wheels, better known today as a motor home.

Perhaps he's where I get my ability to easily and successfully switch jobs.

8   The Power of Prayer

My thinking is interrupted by the ER clerk setting a can of soda on my desk. "Thanks. I owe you one," I say as I snap the top back and take a drink.

"I'm going to hold you to it," she says as she walks away doing a funny little dance. It's good to laugh for a moment so I don't get sucked back into the memories that keep surfacing.

I look down at the drawing. It's becoming so clear and detailed. I know now that the squares on my ceiling that used to torment me every night until my early teens were actually how I focused on escaping the pain and fear of what was happening to me.

I can't believe I got out of there alive. While the rapist covered my mouth with his hand, I remember him saying, "If you yell one more time, I'm going to cover your face with a pillow...If you tell anyone I'm going to tell your mom and dad...If you're not here tomorrow, I'll kill you." All that kept going through my mind was, "It's all my fault...Mom and Dad are going to whip me...and that man is going to kill me tomorrow," because I knew I wasn't ever going to visit the pigeons that roosted on Bob's patio again.

I don't remember how I got out of his house that day, but I do recall turning around, looking at him standing in the doorway of the rental house and hearing him tell me that "I'd better not ever tell anyone." Turning away from him, I walked back across the yard to Flora and Pete's.

Flora gave me a warm hello as I came in the back door, but I hardly answered her and went straight to Lena's bedroom. She followed me, asking if I needed anything. I said "no" as I curled up on the bed. As soon as Flora left, I felt as if I were sinking into a hole that was swallowing the entire bed, with me on it. I threw the covers over my head and began to pray.

I remembered my mother telling me that if I were ever alone and afraid that I should pray and ask God to help me. I must have prayed myself to sleep, because the next thing I remember was waking up to the sound of the back door slamming shut and Flora yelling, "Pete! Pete! Get up. It's Bob. Call an ambulance!"

"What!?" Pete yelled back.

"It's Bob. He's dead."

I heard Flora talking to someone on the phone and then the two of them ran out of the house. I realized it was the next morning and that I had been asleep since yesterday late afternoon. I listened to the ambulance getting closer and closer.

I must have fallen asleep again or passed out, because the next thing I remember I was being shaken awake by Lena.

"Lisa, are you okay?" she asked as she stroked my forehead.

I shook my head 'no.'

"Mom said you aren't feeling well. Do you want something to eat?"

I shook my head 'yes', but I really didn't think I could eat anything.

"Come on then. I'll get you something to eat." Lena pulled the covers back and helped me out of bed. Just walking made my legs hurt and I could barely sit down at the table.

As she handed me a glass of orange juice I heard Flora tell Pete "The police said it looked like he had a heart attack in his sleep."

"When I took Bob a plate of food last night, he seemed fine to me," Ruth said.

I have often wondered what the relationship was between Bob and Ruth. The day I was raped, it was Ruth who had taken me to Bob's house to see the pigeons on his back patio…and then disappeared.

"I'll try to contact his relatives," I heard Flora say.

It was about then that I got really scared. There was no way I was going back there again, and I had prayed with all my might that Bob wouldn't kill me the next day like he'd threatened to. The only thing I thought I could do was pray to God…and now God had killed him to protect me. I was terrified of what I thought I had done.

I remember rocking myself back and forth until I was exhausted and fell asleep. I never told anyone.

As the years passed, my mom never knew the truth about why I cried myself to sleep some nights and was tormented by nightmares of the squares on the ceiling trying to kill me. It got so bad that I began running into my parents room, yelling, "The squares are going to kill me!"

She didn't know what to think as I curled up on her bed shaking so hard that I could hardly talk.

At that time no one knew, not even my mother, that I was raped at six years old. My conscious mind must have forgotten about the incident.

My mom remembers the day Bob died a bit differently. She says that when she came to pick us up, there was an ambulance in the driveway. While talking to Flora and Pete, she saw me standing in the large plate glass window of Flora's living room, my hands pressed flat against the glass and tears streaming down my face. I was wailing so intensely that my breath fogged up the window. Flora pointed at me, saying, "Lisa must have really liked Bob. Do you think she knows what's happened?"

Mirrored Images

© Lisa L. Everly 2006

Conducting the Sun

CHAPTER 9

My Bloody Hands

I continue drawing on my breaks and whenever it's quiet at my desk. It helps pass the time and helps me get through another locked-away secret.

I've probably drawn over thirty pictures sitting at this desk night after night, holding back the tears. It keeps my mind busy as I work things out.

While working here I received a humanitarian award and a couple of other awards. They were supposed to go to the ICU staff, but it was voted that I should receive them instead. Soon, a pay raise followed and I moved to the day shift with weekends off.

The hospital presented me with a special invitation to show my drawings at the D.E.N., a place for employees to show their artwork. I received many wonderful comments about my drawings, and even though most were merely fascinated by their detail, one person guessed at the deeper forces behind their creation.

I recall the woman who'd figured out what I was going through, or at least had a hunch. She said it showed in my drawings.

I had a few of them framed, and they are hanging on my walls at home. Several friends wanted to buy them, but I couldn't part with any, so I made photocopies and gave them to friends who wanted to buy the originals.

Tonight, I'm drawing another: sharp lines and angles with red as the prominent color. The event generating this sketch starts playing out in my mind.

I was thirteen, and my mom and I were on our way to my aunt's house in Norwalk, California. Mom was wearing a beautiful, new fake fur and her hair was all fixed up and piled on top of her head. I don't remember her dressing up much, but today I thought she looked like a movie star.

Mom noticed a young man darting in and out of traffic near the corner of Bellflower Ave. and Alondra Blvd. I could tell she was nervous and heard her say, "I can't believe that guy is jogging in and out of traffic like that."

I looked over toward the man again, and he was right in front of us. A car was approaching quickly in the right-hand turn lane thru the car mirror. I began to roll my window down as fast as I could, thinking I could yell out something that might get his attention. Taking a drink from his pop bottle, he raised his eyes to the sky and didn't even look to see if a car was coming. A moment later, there was only the squeal of tires and the deep, hollow thud of the car hitting his body. Everything seemed to happen in slow motion. His body flew forward, the car swerved with streaks of smoke trailing behind and my hand still rested on the window handle with the words "Watch out!" still locked in my throat.

I jumped out of the truck as mom hurried to park. Kneeling down in the street, I gently lifted the man's head off the hot pavement and out of the growing pool of blood. Mom soon came forward and took off her fake fur coat and handed it to me.

"Put it under his head, Lisa."

I very slowly and carefully placed the coat under him, but the bleeding was heavy and didn't look like it was going to stop.

"Elevate his head," she said.

Mom left me alone for a moment as she circulated among the onlookers, writing down all the information and gathering witnesses. I had seen the other side of this life, but this man's approaching death still scared me as I saw his face begin to turn blue and his eyes flicker. His blood had begun to soak through the fur and seeped down through my fingers and into a puddle on the ground.

"If you can hear me, blink your eyes," I said.

He blinked once.

"Do you believe in God?"

He blinked again.

"The angels are with you. There's an ambulance on the way."

I asked him if he understood me, and I knew that he did because he slowly closed and then reopened his eyes once more.

That was a very busy intersection, and there was a crowd of onlookers all around. I guess I hadn't noticed them before because it seemed like it was just the two of us as I held his head and calmly talked to him. Once I realized there were so many people standing around and staring, I got a bit self-conscious and started to notice what they were saying and doing.

No one else came forward to help, and most didn't even seem concerned. Some casually stood and watched, some muttered about how stupid the man had been to run through traffic and one woman even commented about the damage to the coat.

I heard comments like, "Well, he's not going to make it. Let's get out of here," and, "That's what you get for jaywalking."

The driver of the car came over and looked down at the scene for a moment and then walked back to his Cadillac. Flicking ashes from his cigar, he ran his hand over the dent on the hood and commented about how much it would cost to fix it.

Mom returned and told me, "Stay with him until the ambulance gets here." I did just that. I never stopped talking to him or praying to God, and I never put his head down until the paramedics arrived.

"Thank you, sweetheart. I'll take over now," the paramedic said as he knelt down next to me.

Another paramedic took both my hands in his and began cleaning the blood off of them as I watched the young man being loaded into the waiting ambulance.

Later, the police called my mother and told her he stayed alive just long enough to see his family and the woman he had been engaged to. I wondered why that had to happen since there was a crosswalk just twenty-five feet away.

10   The Look in a Child's Eyes

Arriving at my desk, I notice the sad face of a young woman sitting across from me, and I watch the tears run down her cheeks. I walk over and put my arm around her. She begins to tell me that she only left him alone for a couple of minutes. Just as I hand her a tissue the doctor walks over, takes her hand and says "He's going to be just fine. You may see him now." I smile at her reassuringly and then walk back to my desk.

I know what she has seen and felt through her child's eyes. Having seen it myself, I know it stays with you.

I remember that day as if it were just yesterday. I was ten and we were living in Norwalk at the time.

I awoke as usual, ate my breakfast and got ready for school. It started out as just another day in the life of a fifth grader, as normal or appropriate as my life had been so far.

No one took me to school. I walked the two miles usually by myself, sometimes with my younger sister. That morning I was going to walk by myself, and for some reason I knew I needed to leave right then. Without saying goodbye to my mother I opened the door and began walking down the stairs of the apartment building when I saw a young boy, about three years old. He was riding a tricycle along the side of the pool. After a moment, I saw him swerve a bit and plunge into the cold water of the eight-foot deep end.

It was winter and the pool was closed, but back then they didn't worry about fences or covers.

I threw my books and ran down the two flights of stairs as fast as I could. The little boy, his hand still clutching the handlebars of the trike, was nearly to the bottom of the pool by the time I reached him.

Grabbing the long pool pole, I used the hook on the end to reach down and snag the frame of the trike. Pulling as hard as I could, I brought him back toward the surface as fast as I could.

I knew that if the pole slipped out of my hands, or he let go of the trike, I would have to jump in and save him. I wasn't that good of a swimmer and was especially nervous around the deep end, so I asked God to keep his hands tight on the handlebars until I could get him out.

When I finally got him close enough to reach him, he let go of the trike and grabbed onto my arm as tightly as he could. The trike sank back to the bottom of the pool.

He was hanging onto me for dear life. Shivering from the cold water, he stared into my eyes and didn't say a word. I will never forget the look in his eyes. There was definitely fear there, but also something more that was hard to place yet recognizable.

"you're okay. Everything's going to be all right," I told him.

A moment later, his father came out of one of the

apartments alongside the pool. The boy wasn't about to let go of his safety, and the father had to literally pry his arms from around my neck. As he was pulled away, his eyes seemed to cry out to me for help, but there wasn't anything more I could do. I watched as the father walked off with him, back into the apartment, closing the door behind him.

Sopping wet, I sat on the side of the pool for a moment and tried to put it all together. I knew I had been called to be there to save the child, but for some reason I had the nagging feeling that it wasn't only the pool I needed to save him from. Why had a three-year-old been left by himself, apartment door open and tricycle nearby? Why did the father not say a word to me or the boy, or show any emotion? I sat in silence for a few minutes thinking about all of this.

When I had pulled myself together, I took the pole and fished the trike off the bottom and set it beside the boy's door and then went back upstairs to the apartment to change my clothes.

Mom was worried when she saw me come back all wet. I told her what had happened and she understood and was just glad that both I and the little boy were all right. Later, mom went to the managers and told them what had happened. I never saw the boy again because they moved out shortly after that, but I will never forget what I saw in his eyes. I said a very special prayer for him.

11 The Interrogation

Little by little as my drawings are becoming the object of interest and enthusiasm, I return to my desk and find that items to further the cause have mysteriously appeared. At first I am presented with a blue pen and then a green one, because the staff noticed everything I was drawing was in black and red. But of course everything would be in the same colors as my reports, it's what I had at hand. Each drawing is a random expression of a deliberately buried memory, not an all out artistic expression. I'm not really even aware that I am drawing, let alone what color it is. Each person in their own way wants to help the process and I guess they're thinking color will give me more ways to express myself.

Tonight I find a neatly stacked pile of two red ballpoints, one purple felt tip and a brand new pad of drawing paper, as well as something new—a small bouquet of flowers. They must be from Joyce, since shes been going on about how beautiful my flower drawings are.

As usual, I can't help but wipe a tear away. The generosity and support overwhelm me at times, especially since most people don't even realize what this nightly process really means for me.

I walk my rounds and welcome a few incoming patients to the ER, and then things start to slow for the night and I finally get a chance to put my new pens to work. My mind drifts back to the past, and something starts coming into focus.

I was about twenty years old and had been having such a great day at work. I couldn't wait to get home to tell Mom I had gotten a raise for having the highest-paying collection desk in the office. I had only been working collections for a couple of months, and already I was ahead of the pack. I was thrilled.

Pulling up in the driveway I noticed a beautiful, new sleek black car parked in front of the house. My family couldn't afford such a nice car, so I figured it must be visitors of some importance. I grabbed my empty lunch box, locked the car and rushed inside to see what was going on.

When I opened the door, I noticed two well-dressed men in suits sitting on each end of the couch. As I entered, they both stood and introduced themselves. I don't remember their names, but I certainly remember what came after their names.

"We're Investigators with the Police Department,"

One of them asked me to have a seat so they could ask me a few questions.

I put the things in my arms down on the floor and sat across from them on a hard, straight-backed chair that seemed to have suddenly become totally isolated from the rest of the room.

"Please state your full name and address."

I answered back in an even tone, looking him straight

in the eye. I wasn't afraid. Actually, I was pretty pissed. Not only had my great day and announcement been rail-roaded, but I knew that since I hadn't done anything that would interest the Police this probably had something to do with a family member—most likely my brother or dad. My patience was growing thin.

The two agents continued the questions which mainly consisted of "Where do you work?" and "Who do you asso-ciate with?" After a while, playing twenty questions got old and I finally said, "Can I ask you what this is all about?"

"I will ask the questions," one of them snapped back.

"Do you smoke marijuana?"

"What?" I said.

"Answer the question."

I looked him straight in the eye. "No, I do not." I answered, with not so much as a flinch in my tone.

"Really." The other agent looked over and smiled at my father. The tone and pitch was the type that raised in the middle to let you know that their question was really more a statement of their already determined opinion.

"Really," I said, my eyes still locked on his.

"Look, young lady. You are in serious trouble here. We don't have time for fun and games. I don't like smart asses," he snapped back. I could see his frustration building. I had been through way too much in my life already and it was going to take more than a spiffed-up pencil neck in a new suit to ruffle my feathers.

I guess after that he thought he'd try the silent treat-ment, because he flipped open his note book and started to write. After a moment's composure, he started the interrogation again.

"Have you ever grown marijuana?"

"NO, I have not!" I answered back with a bit more tone in my voice. At this point I started to get a feeling about what might be going on.

Snapping his notebook shut, he stood and said, "Okay, I see you are going to play games with me. So I will be right back with a search warrant."

The two agents walked to the door.

"Mr. Everly, she is not to move from that spot until I get back. Is that understood?"

"Yes, sir!" my dad answered back smartly. He practically saluted.

Once the agents left, Dad rushed to the front window to make sure they were gone and then hurried out the back door. Mom, was cleaning up the kitchen and didn't say a word, so I just sat and waited like I was told.

About thirty minutes passed before Dad hurried in from the back yard. "You didn't see me leave this room. Do you understand?" He said.

"Yeah...sure." I was too busy thinking things through to really hear him. By the time I'd thought about it, I was practically laughing out loud. What kind of police arrive at a scene without a search warrant and then just leave the suspect sitting on the couch while they go get one? The whole thing didn't make sense. I was angry that my Dad was trying to use me as a scapegoat but I should have known nothing changes. Just after Dad told me to mind my own business, the agents returned with the search warrant.

"Come with me, Lisa," one of them said.

"You too, Mr. Everly."

"Yes, sir!" My dad snapped.

As we entered the back yard, one of the agents walked

over to the corner and said, "Where are the marijuana plants that were here just thirty minutes ago?"

Everyone turned to look at me and I just shrugged, trying not to laugh.

"How would I know?" I said. "I've been sitting in the same chair ever since you guys left, just like you told me to."

Visibly frustrated and angry, the agent turned to Dad and said, "There were plants here. I showed them to you, Mr. Everly. What happened to them?"

"I don't know. I saw them, too," Dad said.

"Lisa, do you know growing marijuana is illegal? If I come back here again, and I will, and I find marijuana of any sort, I will arrest you. Do you understand what I'm telling you?"

"I understand, but…" Before I could say anything else, Dad was telling me to go to the house. We were "going to have a talk about this."

I was mad as hell.

Walking back to the house, I almost turned around and told them about what Dad had been up to for years, but they were rude to me so I figured they didn't deserve any information and could face the embarrassment of the mistake they'd made.

I had no idea about the plants back there. Dad had staked claim to the back yard and I never had reason to go back there. It had only been two weeks since I'd moved in with my folks and during that time all I did was sleep and work, trying to get enough money for my own place.

Once I got the money I was out of there, and I never forgot how my Dad was willing to let me take the fall. I guess he figured they'd just slap my hand since it would have been my first offense, but that was a pretty big assumption.

As the present works its way free from the past, I think to myself, "Little wonder I have trouble trusting people." Funny, so many people say I'm the one person they would trust with their lives. I guess that supports my belief that if it's been done to you, that doesn't mean your likely to do it to others. The term "If you can't beat them, join them," shouldn't be in anyone's vocabulary.

12 My Day
at the Beauty Salon

"Hey, Lisa. Want to sign Dr. Jackson's birthday card?" Trish asks.

"Sure," I say. Taking the card, I find a spot between ten other birthday wishes and ad my quip about his advancing years. "Here you go."

Even as a kid, I never liked to celebrate my birthday. My younger sister loved parties and all the hoopla but to this day I still don't.

I look down at the flowers I'm drawing and drop my pen on the desk. Jumping up, I begin to wipe away the tears that I'm losing control over. I decide that an early perimeter check is needed.

I remember meeting a guy named Rick, who worked at the truck stop fuel station, a few months before I turned nineteen. He was quite a bit older and had a pleasant personality. He seemed nice enough. One day when I was with my cousin, he asked me out to dinner and I accepted.

We started dating, and I thought he was really good to me. He bought me a car, helped me pay my rent and even bought groceries sometimes.

Soon, my birthday rolled around. We had been dating for about four months, and he asked if I would like to have my hair done for my special day. I had only been in a "real" beauty salon once before in California, so I didn't really know what to expect. I thought that getting a professional haircut in a fancy salon would be wonderful. I was really looking forward to going.

"I'll pick you up tomorrow," he said.

We drove all over Muskogee, looking for his friend's salon. While we traveled up one street and down another for what seemed like a very long time, I began to think I was seeing the same streets over and over again. However, the longer we drove around and the more turns we took, I was sure that indeed we were going around in circles. The tire store with the brightly colored sale sign and the car lot with the balloons on all the antennas were unmistakable, telltale signs.

I had only lived there a little while and I didn't know my way around, especially in the old parts of downtown. I drove to work and back, and to the grocery store, and that was usually the extent of it. Nothing looked familiar to me, aside from the repeating landmarks, on this carousel I was on.

After driving around for an hour, we finally pulled up in front of the salon. The neighborhood was run down, and there was an empty lot to one side and an alley running along the back. The building was old, and the tinkle-tinkle of a bell announced our arrival as Rick walked me inside. It definitely wasn't what I had expected.

"I'll be back for you later," he said. "Enjoy yourself."

"I will," I said.

Writing my name, address and phone number in the

guest register on the counter, I looked around and noticed there was no one else in the shop. The hairdresser wasn't even there to greet me.

"Come on back, Lisa," a man's voice said from somewhere behind a screen.

I walked back and sat down in one of the chairs.

While I sat looking around, the man came up behind me. The chair suddenly jerked as he pumped it up to the height he wanted.

Still standing behind me, we chatted for a while about how I wanted my hair cut, but then the direction of our conversation changed.

"Hey," he said, "I'm having a special. Have you ever had a facial?"

"No, never," I answered.

"Well then, today is your lucky day! You get a free facial with your cut," he said. "It will really clean your face and make you feel really good," he added. "So, how about it? You want it?"

"Will it take very long?" I asked.

"No."

"Okay then. Sounds good," I said.

He mixed up something behind me. I could hear the spoon clacking away at the sides of the bowl as he told me, "Now close your eyes."

Spreading the mixture over my face like birthday cake frosting, he stepped in front of me, saying "No matter what, keep your eyes closed."

Placing some kind of patch over each eye, he added, "This stuff will burn your eyes really bad if you open them, so keep 'em closed."

Just then, the phone rang in the back of the shop and

I heard him walk away to answer it. I could hear him talking in low tones to the person on the other end, and then the click of the handset. I don't remember hearing him walk back toward me, but a moment later he was standing behind me again, leaning over my shoulder, close to my ear.

"I want you to be very still. Don't move, yell or try to stop me."

It was then I felt something cold and hard against my neck. I knew at that moment I was in very serious trouble, and the little voice that had been trying to get my attention all morning had been right. I might not make it through this one.

He moved in front of me, and I felt him grab my waist and pull me to the edge of the chair. While his hand unzipped my pants and pulled them down to my knees, I kept my eyes shut as tightly as I could—and I prayed.

Then he raped me.

"Now see, that wasn't so bad, was it?"

"No," I answered in a calm and convincing voice.

"Good. We're going to do it again," he said.

I figured I still had a chance, and I was going to play it through with all the strength and showmanship I could muster. No tears or pleas for mercy. I was going to play the game and I was going to walk away—alive! I had come too far to be just another nameless victim found buried in a shallow grave. God hadn't brought me through everything in my life so far for it to end here, like this.

I heard a car pull up in the alley behind the shop. The back door creaked open, and we were no longer alone in the room.

The scene was repeated over and over. In all, I counted

five different colognes and five different pairs of hands,
Five times I told myself I could hold on a little longer.

Then, at last, I heard the back door squeak open and
closed again, and the vehicle in the alley drove off.

Once again we were alone and he was in front of me.

"Let's do it one more time, okay?"

It was really a statement more than a question, because
of course I had no choice in the matter. His even asking
me seemed ridiculous.

He was really getting into it. I could tell because he
started talking to me. It seemed like he wasn't going to kill
me, and I was going to get out of there alive.

He pulled my pants back up as far as he could and
said, "I really like you, Lisa. You can't tell anyone about
this, because if you do I will know about it and I won't be
too happy...and neither will you." He said that line with a
cold and steady tone, letting me know that if I talked, my
luck would run out fast.

"So, let's just be friends," he said, "and I'll give you free
haircuts from now on, if you'd like. How's that sound?"

"Sounds like a deal to me," I answered with the most
believable smile I could fake.

He then took me to the sink, helped me wash the mask
off my face and then led me to the hair washing station.

"You have such beautiful hair," he said as he ran his
fingers through it.

He wrapped a towel around my head and walked me
back to the chair, where he proceeded to cut and style my
hair.

Just as he finished, Rick came in and sat down.

"She's all yours, Rick," he said.

Rick paid and we left, the doorbell tinkling a friendly

goodbye.

Back in the car with Rick, my mind was racing. The whole thing was too organized to have been a random assault. This was well planned and well orchestrated, and I was going to have to keep up the charade with Rick, too. I knew I was not out of danger yet. I had to keep playing their game because I believed Rick was also involved.

"So, do you like your hair?" he asked.

"I love it."

"I'll drop you off at your place. I have to go to work."

After he dropped me off I began to sob, and all of the fear and panic from the last few hours crashed down on me in one heavy blow. My resolve worn to the ground. I sunk to my knees and wept. I thanked God that I was still alive. In the back of my mind, I didn't think I would be walking out of that salon alive.

I couldn't tell anyone what had happened. The stylist said they would know if I told, and I believed him by the way he said it. Something that organized and involving that many men could reach into the very places I might try to hide—maybe even into the police department. I had no idea who I could trust or talk to; previous experience had shown me that. I had to take care of myself, even if it meant running and not looking back.

A friend helped me pack my belongings. As we loaded everything we could into the car Rick had bought me, a man from the car dealership walked up.

"Young lady, I'm repossessing this vehicle," he said. "Rick hasn't made one payment on this car since he bought it. I'm sorry, and I hope you'll figure out you're in the wrong company."

That, indeed, was the height of understatement. Yes, I

had figured that one out.

He drove away with the car, leaving my possessions piled on the front porch. We started again with my friends car, loaded everything in and drove away. I didn't look back.

I moved back to the small town I'd just left a few months earlier. I was hoping it was far enough away to be safe, but one day I saw Rick in traffic behind me. I don't know if he saw me or not, but I raced forward, changed lanes and zig-zagged through alleys and side streets.

I have since gone looking for the hair salon, but to this day I haven't been able to find it. As clearly as I remember what happened, you would think I could remember where it was. But the twists and turns he took me on to get there have made it impossible to find.

It was always those who appeared to be good to me who let me down and set me up for pain and failure. One night I had a dream that gave me the message to not be afraid of what I could see, that as long as I could see clearly I would do the right thing and stay away from danger. The dream warned me to be aware of what I could *not* see in others. Those who seem pure and good in the eyes of man don't always seem so in the eyes of God.

Tailfeathers Jazz Band

© Lisa L. Everly 2006

Twizzle, Dink and Que

© Lisa L. Everly 2006

13   Day at the Beach

Looking down at my watch, I see it's time to finally go home. Thank heaven. Enough is enough, and my facade is wearing thin. I carefully place my notebook, sketch pad and pens back in their case and turn my desk over to the next shift.

"It's been a pretty uneventful evening so far," I say to the next guard. "Have a good one."

Gathering my motorcycle helmet and gloves, I head for the door. As I step out into the parking lot the fresh, crisp air hits my face and a wave of relief overcomes me. I let out a long, deep sigh as tears form in the corners of my eyes. Now I can take a moment for myself, before I have to stuff it all back in to play my next role.

At home I have many roles: head of the household, breadwinner and bill payer. It's been hard making ends meet with a mortgage on a new home.

I also play landlord to the roommate I took on in order to make ends meet. This, too, hasn't been easy since she's fighting her own battles. I try to help, but it's so hard just making it through the day with my own struggles. I try to just collect the rent and retreat to my room on the nights she comes home drunk, wanting to take out her anger on someone.

There is also my role as the tough-yet-supportive sister. In a final, desperate act of love I welcomed my younger sister to my home in Oregon to sober up from meth and alcohol. I have always been teased by my family as being the goody–goody or the saint, but when they're in trouble they come to me and I always help, even when I can barely help myself.

And as always, there is my role of the understanding and supportive daughter to my mother, complete with phone calls at all hours relating messages of abandonment and abuse. How many times would I have to listen to her say that my Dad had run off again or had threatened her? All I can do is just offer my ear on the other end of the line and say "Yes, Mom" and "Everything will be okay, Mom."

No place offers any peace for me right now, except maybe on the back of my motorcycle.

When I reach my bike, a big smile comes across my face. Seeing the shiny chrome and deep purple paint relaxes me instantly and right now, life is good. Nothing in this world makes me feel as good as riding my motorcycle. The freedom it brings helps me forget what's going on in my life; unfortunately, it never allows me to outrun it. I laugh to myself about the bumper sticker I have read so many times: "Don't drive faster than your Angels can fly." I think I should sell my own, which would read "My Angels fly pretty darn fast!"

I unlock the front fork and wonder if anyone will ask me how my day was when I get home.

As I drive through town, the headlights of oncoming

cars flash in my eyes and I remember another time when the light flashed in my eyes, a time when I was shifting between light and darkness, heaven and earth. That day, an angel came again to save me.

I was fourteen, and my mother's youngest brother, Uncle George, and her oldest sister's son, Johnny, came to visit us that summer.

I couldn't wait to see Johnny who was only three months older than I was. Mom said they would be there the next morning, and I tossed and turned all night in anticipation of their arrival.

A couple of days later, Johnny saw my surfboard in the garage.

"Hey, Lisa. Can you teach me to surf?" he asked.

"Sure," I said.

Johnny and I finally talked Uncle George into taking us down to Huntington Beach for the day. George wasn't all that thrilled about the idea because he had never learned to swim and was afraid of the water, but we assured him there would probably be lots of pretty women in bikinis to watch if he didn't want to go in the water. He agreed.

With less than an hour-and-a-half drive from Bellflower to Huntington Beach, the time seemed to fly by. We finally found a parking spot and opened the doors to the truck. Johnny, yelled out "Woo-hoo!" and run toward the sand. "Hurry up, Lisa!" he yelled back.

George helped me unload the surfboards and the cooler and we followed after Johnny who was already knee deep in the surf, arms outstretched and swaying back and forth as if he were coming in on a curl.

"Hey, wait for me!" I yelled as I set the cooler down at the base of lifeguard station eighteen.

Once we got in the water, I noticed that Johnny kept paddling further and further out into the surf. I tried to keep him close to me and in the shallows until he got the hang of things, but he just wouldn't listen.

I went out as far as I was going to go when all of a sudden: *Here comes Johnny!* He'd caught a wave and was headed straight for me. The water was over my head, and he had no control over the board. There was little I could do to get out of the way.

Thud.

And then the darkness came.

All I can remember is that I was rolling and rolling. Over and over I turned in the water, not sure which direction was up and which was down. The only indication of above and below was the light from the surface, which flashed past my eyes as I tossed and turned in the surf. But that was beginning to fade away, and I was surrounded by nothing but darkness.

Continuing on this way for what seemed like an eternity, I closed my eyes and thought "God, if it's my turn to go, I'm ready; but if it's not, please help me." It was up to God now. I couldn't hold my breath a moment longer and I was fighting for my life like never before, but soon let go of all the remaining air I held in my lungs. It seemed the fight for my life was just about over. That, by far, is the worst feeling I have ever experienced.

Opening my eyes, I was surrounded by the brightest, warmest light, and I knew my angel was with me. I have never felt safer than I did in that moment. Everything turned into a peaceful, slow motion, and I knew I wasn't alone anymore. I couldn't see a face or hear a voice as before, but the brightest and safest light flowed around me in the water like sheets of silk in slow motion. The angel had come to save me again.

In the light I was calm and peaceful, I lost all fear when I heard a voice say "Be still". My body completely relaxed into the arms of the angel, and the rolling turbulence stopped. I knew everything was going to be okay.

"Do you want to stay or do you want to go back?" my angel asked.

"My mother will miss me and she needs me, I want to go back."

When I came to, I was standing in knee-deep water gasping for air. In front of me sat a beautiful black woman wearing a white shirt and blue jeans rolled up to her knees. She sat alone, quietly in the sand with her ankles crossed and her hands wrapped around her knees. There was something very special about her, more than just her beauty. I will never forget her smile.

I had not yet perceived what had just happened and I was a bit confused.

"Is this heaven?" I asked her.

"Where did you come from?" she said as she got up and started to walk toward me.

"I was drowning and an angel saved me."

"I believe you sweetheart, I just hope they will," she said as she helped me out of the water.

"Where are all the people? I asked.

"There are some people down there," she said, pointing to a spot way down the beach.

I began walking toward them. When I finally found my uncle, I was so tired I couldn't take one more step. I collapsed into the sand.

"Where did you go?" he asked.

"The surfboard Johnny was riding hit me on the head, and I was drowning."

"Drowning!" Uncle George yelled. "That's all I'd need, to have to tell your mom that you drowned! Go get Johnny and let's go."

We gathered up our things and climbed into the truck to go home. I can't believe Johnny didn't notice that I'd disappeared. Everyone was really quiet on the way home, and I told my uncle he didn't have to say anything to Mom about what had happened. To this day I don't know if he ever said anything. I eventually did. As usual, she understood.

I went back years later to Huntington Beach, found lifeguard station eighteen and walked down the highway to where I had come out of the water that day. It was nearly a mile away.

14   A Fear Overcome

My body pushes against the wind as I move my way through traffic on my beautiful purple motorcycle. For the first time in a long while, my mind is clear and calm. I start composing a song in my head and jazzy blues tunes begin rolling by, inspired by the rhythm of my tires on the pavement. I can visualize my cartoon character Dazz, who has become a favorite with the staff at work, blowing musical bubbles on her saxophone. Along with the rest of her musical family, she is by far the coolest cartoon character I have drawn yet.

I'm not ready to go home yet, so I pull into the market to grab a little something for dinner. I don't really feel like cooking, but I know I need to eat. I can't believe I'm choosing to go into a big supermarket rather than go home. There was a time in my life when it was all I could do to enter a store with a crowd of people. For years I struggled with it.

Pulling into the parking lot of Fred Meyer, I glide to a stop next to the front door, take off my helmet and gloves and lean the bike on its stand. It's a warm evening and a large number of people are hurrying in and out. Some seem happy, some seem hurried. Parents call to their children who are lagging behind, and others search through their pockets for their car keys.

My mind journeys back, as I picture myself years earlier, standing just off the sidewalk. I was frozen with fear, too determined to turn and run and too frightened to go inside. With hands clenched tightly, sweat beading on my forehead and my heart racing ninety miles an hour, I stood motionless, carrying on the same conversation with myself that I'd had a hundred times.

"Why can't you just go in and get what you want like everyone else?" I thought.

"You're not going to let this get to you."

"You are going to go inside, and you are going to beat this thing once and for all," I scolded myself.

I don't know how they started, but I fought with panic attacks and a fear of crowds for a good share of my childhood and early adulthood. It was one of the things that kept me from going to school.

Perhaps I started to fear people because I had been hurt too many times, whether it had been the man who raped me at six or the kids who taunted and harassed me as the new kid in school, or even the teachers who ridiculed me. Maybe it was because throughout my life the places that were supposed to be safe turned out not to be and the people who were supposed to look out for me didn't. I just wanted to be by myself. In a crowd, there were just too many things pushing in on me, and I felt like I was going to die or go crazy.

Reminding myself that's in the past, I walk inside. The first thing I need is a loaf of bread.

As I walk through the store I remember that as a child my mother would ask me to go to the store for her to get a loaf of bread and maybe some milk, fruit, cigarettes and a soda. She knew exactly how much the items cost, and that was the exact amount of money she would send me away with. I would make my way to the store with her list and end up standing in front of the doors too frightened to go inside, yet more frightened of returning home empty handed. I didn't want to disappoint her, and I didn't want her to find out her little girl couldn't do something all the other kids did for their parents. Going to the store alone was a rite of passage and a privilege.

While the big, less expensive grocery store was overwhelming, the little mom and pop market on the way there was not. I could gather enough courage to go inside because there was never too many people in there. The problem was that the money my mother gave me was never enough to buy what she'd asked for.

Resourceful child that I was, I usually had a bit of extra money from mowing lawns or selling things at the flea market, so I would simply go to the smaller store and make up the difference without my mother ever knowing. When she finally figured it out, she wasn't angry with me—she just didn't really understand why I did it.

I wasn't about to let this phobia go on and ruin my life, so I made up my mind that I wasn't going to give in to the fear anymore. I really wanted to know why this was happening to me, and most of all I wanted to know how to stop it.

"You can beat this if you only put your mind to it. What's wrong with you?" I would think to myself.

"There is nothing to be afraid of," I would remind

myself. "God is looking out for you." And then I would try again and again, as many times as it took. It didn't happen overnight, but the panic attacks did eventually stop. Since then, I've even held jobs inside of malls and other places with crowds of people. Like all difficulties in my life, there was no other option but to get through it, and I did.

I set the bread in my basket and walk down the next aisle to get a bottled coffee and a package of lunch meat from the deli. Who'd ever thought I'd be killing time shopping?

I laugh to myself and smile as a woman and a small child pass me in the aisle.

Not able to take much with me on the bike, I call it quits and head for the register. I set the items down and hand the cashier my money and Rewards card. Yes, determination has had its rewards for me.

Back in the parking lot, I arrange my groceries for the remainder of the trip home, put on my helmet and start the engine. It's time to go home, and I hope it's quiet when I get there. The light turns green and I'm gone.

I pass a park and find myself driving beside a long, dark, wrought-iron fence. Its evenly spaced bars are hypnotizing as they seem to turn everything behind them into a slow-motion movie. It reminds me of the distortions in our perception that alter how we see the world. I remember looking through bars like these when I was nine years old. And as it happens, I had gone to the grocery store that day, too.

15   Car at the Curb

At that time I loved walking to the Tic-Toc market, which was about two blocks from our house. I would get myself a few pieces of candy and a cola and some smokes for Mom. If I had a bit of extra change, I'd splurge and get myself an orange sherbet pop-up. Those were the best.

On that particular day, I finished my chores and asked Mom if she wanted me to get her anything from the corner store. Putting in her usual request, she handed me a couple of dollars and I headed for the door.

"Be back in a few minutes, Mom," I called to her as I pushed the front door open and skipped down the stairs to the sidewalk.

About halfway between our house and the store was a Christian school. I walked past the tall, dark, metal fence and saw the kids inside playing hopscotch and rolling balls along the grass, while their teachers watched and talked in groups of two or three. At that age, I didn't know the difference between public and private schools, but I knew that none of the kids in the neighborhood went to that school, so there must be something different about it.

Even the teachers looked different, walking around the playground in their long dresses.

The kids looked like they were having fun, but I was still glad to be on the outside of the fence, on my own and walking to the store. It was just too hard always being the new kid in school and trying to fit in and make new friends.

Continuing on, I hopped across the cracks in the sidewalk. "Step on a crack, break your mama's back," I hummed in my head. Suddenly, I stopped myself dead in my tracks. The air felt cold, like I'd just walked past an open refrigerator, and I had chills all over me and goose bumps on my arms. I looked around, thinking I might catch someone or something sneaking up behind me, but there wasn't anything there out of the ordinary: just children, teachers, a quiet street and one parked car.

Everything looked normal, but I knew when that feeling came over me, something might happen. I didn't really understand the significance of my these premonitions yet, I was old enough to have figured out that not everybody had them and that they were often followed by something unusual.

Slowly, I began to walk toward the store. Still looking around, I didn't see anything out of the ordinary. As I passed the parked car I glanced in the passenger side window. Nothing seemed odd about it. It was just a run-of-the-mill, dark-brown sedan with the windows rolled up.

Relieved yet confused, I passed the car and the feeling faded.

"Onward!" I yelled. With ice cream on my mind, I ran down the sidewalk forgetting all about the cracks and my mother's safety.

Reaching the big, four-lane intersection, I looked both ways, then both ways again. I took a deep breath, looked both ways once more and ran for it. I was always relieved when I made it to the other side.

"Hey, Lisa! I haven't seen you in a few days. How 'ya been, kid-o?" the store clerk said as he closed the register.

"Yesterday I hit a home run at the park," I said, smiling as I reached in and grabbed an orange pop-up.

"Wow! What team do you play on?" he asked.

"Well, girls can't play on the team, but they let me practice with them."

"How come you can't play baseball with the boys? You're as good as they are, right?"

"Yeah," I said with a hint of resentment. I knew I was actually better than most of them.

I asked for the smokes and the cola and handed him my money.

"See 'ya later," I said as I took the bag and pushed the change into my pocket.

Once outside, I crossed the highway again and started back toward home. The closer I got to the school, the slower I began to walk. The feeling was coming back, and this time I found myself focusing on the brown sedan parked at the curb in front of the playground.

From somewhere in the back of my mind the message came to me. *He's dead.*

I looked through the rear window and could see the back of someone's head in the driver's seat. I knew the message was probably right, but I had to be sure.

I walked to the driver's side window and saw a man with his head back and his eyes closed. When I tapped on the window, he didn't move. I pressed my face to the glass to see if his chest was moving. It confirmed what I already knew: he was dead.

I started searching for clues. There was no gun, no knife and no blood. It didn't look like anyone had killed him or that he'd killed himself, so what had happened? As much as I wanted to figure it out, I knew that I needed to let someone know what I'd found.

Looking past the man, through the car window, I saw the children playing and the teacher standing in her long dress. I knew I needed to tell her what I'd found, but I also knew I needed to do it without frightening the children.

Walking around the car and back onto the sidewalk, I went to the fence and called out between the bars.

"Excuse me, lady! Hello? Excuse me!"

She didn't hear me but the children next to her did. One of them pulled on her dress and pointed toward me. She looked up and walked toward me with a couple of the children following.

"What is it, sweetheart?" she asked.

"Can I talk to you...alone?"

She turned and directed the children back to where they'd come from.

"Yes. What can I help you with?" she said as she returned.

I pointed and said, "There's a dead man in that car."

She looked over at the car and asked, "How do you know that?"

"Because he's not breathing."

"Can you wait right here?"" she said a bit frantically. "I'll go get someone."

"I can't stay long. My mother might get worried."

"Okay" she said, heading toward the building in a hurry.

A few moments later, she and another woman returned and asked me where the man was.

I pointed to the car. "He's right there."

Then she asked if I lived in the neighborhood. I pointed and told her that I lived in the big yellow house down the street.

"I called the police and they're on their way," she said.

I thanked her and continued walking home, even though I really wanted to stay and find out what happened.

Forgetting to wipe my feet, I rushed in to the house and told Mom what had happened. I told her the man was just down the street in front of the school and that the ambulance was coming.

As I went to my room, I heard the front door shut. When Mom returned, I asked her if the police and ambulance showed up and she told me they did and everything was all right. There was a knock at the door, and Mom told me to stay in the kitchen. I heard her talking with a police officer at the front door who was asking about what I'd told her and if I was okay with what I'd just seen. He was concerned about me, but Mom reassured him that I was fine. When she returned to the kitchen, she told me the police officer wanted her to tell me I had done a "good job" and that the man had probably died of a heart attack.

She gave me a big hug and I headed out the door wondering if he was going to Heaven.

Two weeks later, I assisted the police in catching a guy who'd committed grand theft auto. I had watched him race into the parking lot behind our house and jump out of the car, leaving the door open and the engine running.

As he ran down the street I followed him, staying close enough that I didn't lose him, but far enough behind so he wouldn't notice I was following him. When he ducked into a house, I took note of the address and ran home, where I told my mother to call the police. When they arrived I told them where the car was, what the man looked like and the address where he was hiding. A little while later, they came back down the street. With the suspect in handcuffs, they loaded him into the back of the patrol car.

I guess I was working security even then.

16   Caught Red-Handed

I make the last few turns into my neighborhood and realize it's time to pull myself together and see what the atmosphere is like at home. I'm hoping for a peaceful night without any drama, but those are few and far between anymore. What I wouldn't give for a hot cup of tea and a long soak in the tub.

Gearing down, I glide into the driveway, hit the garage-door opener and come to a stop with the door settling shut behind me. I look up, and my sister Janie is standing there with a hot cup of tea.

"Mmmm. Just what I need, sis. Thanks."

"Actually Lisa, I want to talk to you about something," she says in a tone that hints of frustration, anger and apprehension.

"Okay, but can you at least give me a second to get my helmet off?"

Following Janie into the house I notice Terry, my roommate, lying on the floor and snoring like a grizzly bear.

"How long has she been out?" I ask.

"Well, that's what I want to talk to you about."

I can tell Janie is trying to speak slowly and stay calm, but it isn't working very well. I wonder how long she'll be able to keep it up.

"Terry's been drinking all day! She drank herself into a fucking frenzy, turned on your stereo as loud as it would go and then started banging on your drum set out in the garage. She thought she was a fucking rock star and she drove me absolutely crazy! Then, I came out of the bathroom and found her passed out cold right here on the floor." Janies says, waving her finger up and down as if she's a mother scolding a child.
"She hasn't moved since one o'clock."

I look at my watch and see that it's now six forty-five.

"Okay, Can you grab me a cold towel?" I ask.

"What do you mean? You're going to help her! I say dump her on her bed and let her sleep it off. She's the one who broke the rules!" Janie says with a tone of disbelief.

"Well, if it were you…and it has been…I'd be doing the same."

She returns with the cold towel, and I begin trying to wake Terry up. After a while, she starts to come to, and I help her to bed.

After straightening up the house and eliminating all traces of the afternoon's fiasco, I sit down at the table, where Janie is sipping her tea. Tears begin to run down her face as she searches for the words to apologize. I know she realizes it wasn't so long ago that she was the one lying on the floor, passed out from her addiction.

I come around the table and give her a big hug.

"It's okay sis," I say gently.

"Sometimes how I choose to react may seem a bit strange, but it's just the right thing to do. I know you're upset with Terry, but don't forget that you came here only a couple of months ago and were in the same situation."

Janie lowers her eyes and stares into her tea, giving the cup a slow stir with the spoon. I notice her hands are shaking and wonder if it's the emotions she's feeling or the lingering effects of the meth.

"I stayed by your side as you dealt with the demons from your withdrawals, and it wasn't a pretty sight. I guess you had to be on this end of it in order to see that. You tossed and turned, talked in your sleep and practically crawled out of your skin, and I made sure every time you woke up there was something for you to eat and drink. I let you know I was there with you and that you weren't going through it alone or with someone you couldn't trust. And during that time, not once did Terry ever question what I was doing for you."

Janie nods in agreement.

"I remember lying beside you, asking God to help you with your addiction and to give you the strength to stay straight so one day you'd be able see your kids again…and he has." I smile and look into her eyes, laying my hand on hers. She knows there's still a long road in front of her—and so do I.

"Sometimes we do things we would never have thought we'd have to do, but sometimes that's just the way it is."

Janie wipes her tears away and tells me that if it weren't for me she would be dead by now. I tell her that's not true and that if it weren't for God she wouldn't have made it here to a safe place where she could recover.

"I want you to know how proud I am of you. Meth destroys a person's heart and soul, robbing them of not only their family and home, but also their spirit and connection to God. You are doing a remarkable thing that not everyone manages to do, even with all the support or money in the world. You are pulling yourself out of the darkness, finding your way, your spirit and your God. You're getting off meth, pretty much by yourself. It's a great accomplishment, and I hope you stick with it for your sake and your kids.'"

Now my eyes are filling with tears as well, and we sit and look at each other in silence. So much has happened.

I think back to the day I picked Janie up from the bus station in Portland, Oregon. It was supposed to be a simple two-day trip from California, but it took her over a week, since she repeatedly fell asleep or wandered away from the bus stop, missing her next departure. Sleeping through the stop at the Eugene depot, she found herself in Portland. I decided it would be easier to drive the two-and-a-half hours north, rather than trying to get her on another bus the next day.

When I arrived at the station I walked right past her. Even when I heard someone say, "Lisa! Hey, Lisa!" and I turned around, I still didn't recognize her. Janie didn't look like Janie anymore: not in her face, clothing or the way she talked. This was a different Janie than the one I knew.

The last time I had seen her she'd been working as a model, but that day, seeing her sunken eyes and pale, withered skin, all I wanted to do was cry. Walking toward her, I did my best to hold back the tears and put on a big smile. There would be time for tears later.

"Glad to see you, sis. Let's go home," I said, giving her a big hug.

On the drive home, I kept looking at her in the rear-view mirror. I wiped away the tears as I wondered if my little sister was still inside that body somewhere, and If I'd

ever get her back. She rambled on pointlessly about one
thing or another for the entire two-and-a-half hour drive.
As I listened, my hope grew dimmer. I remember that I just
kept smiling.

But that was months ago, and now I see my little sister
sitting in front of me, her eyes bright and her mind clear.
We've both been through a lot today, so it's time to lighten
the mood. I reach for her cup and ask if she'd like more tea.

"Yeah. Sounds great," she says.

"You know, Lisa, Mom has told me stories about when
you were little. You've done some amazing things and had
a lot of freaky things happen to you. Would you tell me
about one? Maybe something recent. Things still happen
to you, right?"

"Oh, yeah. Things still happen. Give me a minute and
I'll tell you what happened here last year."

Finishing up the dishes, I light a candle and turn off
all the lights. Janie and I take the big pillows off the couch,
grab a blanket and lie down on the floor head to head.
I close my eyes and begin telling her about the night I
caught the car vandals. I haven't told many people this
story, but I bet the guys down at the police station have.
These vandals had been tormenting them for the better
part of two years by breaking into cars, trashing them and
taking whatever they could get their hands on.

"Okay. I am going to tell you about the last time I
was summoned by the angel, but you can't ask any questions until I'm done. Then I'll answer whatever you want.
Okay?"

"Okay," she says, trying to sound serious. I know she's
as anxious as a kid at summer camp waiting for the counselor to tell a ghost story. All we're missing is a flashlight

held under my chin. There are no tall tells though. All my stories are true.

My mind takes me back to almost a year ago.

It was just after dinner, and I'd decided to work in the garden for a while since I'd neglected it for over a week. The weeds were taking over, and I was on a mission to stop them. I always had an immaculate yard, and I love gardening.

My girlfriend at the time, Kim, was barbecuing steaks on the grill. Schultz, my German shepherd, watched her every move from his own miniature version of our house, which I had recently built for him.

I was home, working in my garden with my dog nearby and a juicy steak on the way. All was right with the world. But then that gray feeling started to come over me, and I knew something was going to happen. I didn't know what right then, so I continued to pull weeds while paying close attention to my surroundings, knowing things would become clear in time.

"Steaks are done!" Kim yelled out.

I went inside, ate dinner and carried on as if nothing were happening. Kim didn't need to know anything yet, or maybe at all. I generally handle these things on a need-to-know basis.

After clearing the table, I told Kim I was going to take a shower and turn in early. Tomorrow was my day off, and I had planned on riding my motorcycle to the beach and taking pictures all day. I was really looking forward to it, but the anticipation was getting overshadowed by the lingering feeling that something was going on.

Getting into bed, I reminded myself not to be annoyed or confused that nothing had happened yet, and that I should be thankful for the advanced notice.

I slept very peacefully that night and wasn't worried or scared about what I might be called to do. I was very calm and let things happen in the order they normally did. As I slept, I could feel the essence of the angel coming closer.

I don't remember Kim coming to bed, but when I finally awoke to the sound of the elevator chime at three twenty-one in the morning, she was there sleeping beside me. I sat straight up in bed, wide awake and scanning every inch of the room with my eyes and spiritual senses.

I determined I wasn't in any immediate danger, and then I got up to check the rest of the house.

When my feet touched the floor, Kim woke up and said, "Where are you going?"

"Stay here," I whispered to her. "I'll be right back." Going over to the window, I parted the blinds and looked out into the darkness.

"Kim, don't follow me and don't turn on any lights. I'll let you know if you need to do anything," I said as I opened the bedroom door.

I could tell Kim wanted to protest and follow along behind me, but she managed to control her curiosity and stayed in bed. When this happens it must be confusing and I try to take that into consideration.

I moved on to the guest room, looking out the windows there, and then into the kitchen. Still nothing seemed out of the ordinary as I looked through the sliding glass door into the back yard. My eyes scanned all the dark corners, and my senses felt for any danger. None there.

The house was on a corner and I checked one of the side streets, Colton, from the dining room window. Nothing.

I had pretty much run out of places to check. The house was clear, Kim was all right, the back yard was fine. Even Schultz was quietly sleeping in his dog house. God had tested me once with a false alarm so I'd know which feelings were real and which were not, and I knew this was the real thing. I moved on to the living room, which faced Austin Way.

When I reached the living room window the fuzzy, gray feeling shot up about ten points. Bingo! No doubt about it. I got down on my knees and parted the blinds. Looking in all directions, I saw nothing except darkness and a few parked cars along the curb in each direction. All I could do was sit and wait.

After about five minutes, Kim came into the living room and asked, "What are you doing!?"

"What does it look like I'm doing!?" I whispered with irritation in my voice. "Don't turn on any lights!"

"Why? What's going on?" she asked in a much less sarcastic and more concerned tone.

"I'm not sure yet, but something is going to happen, and it's going to happen right out there."

"What do you mean something is going to happen?"

"Remember I told you that sometimes I hear a chime that sounds like an elevator bell and when that happens I know the angel has come to tell me that I am going to be a part of something, to help someone or witness something? That happened tonight, and now I'm just waiting and watching for whatever it is."

Kim seemed satisfied with that explanation, and I told her to get down on her knees and look out the window with me. Kneeling in silence, we waited.

"Did you see that? A truck just pulled up to the curb

down there on Colton," I said, pointing into the darkness.

"It's pitch black down there. I don't see anything."

"I do. An older-model pickup just pulled in down there with its lights off."

Before she could tell me again that it was way too dark to see anything, I added that there were three guys in the cab and they were going to break into cars.

"Watch," I said. "Two of them are going to get out and walk down here to the house and up to my van. One is going to try and break into it while another guy stands watch at the back."

Kim raised up a little higher and parted the blinds more as she struggled to see what I was describing.

"I still don't see anything." Then a second later, "Look, you're right! They just lit up cigarettes!"

The glow stood out like beacons and Kim was ecstatic about finally seeing it for herself. I considered saying, "I told you so," but decided not to. It wasn't about being right, it was about knowing what one can see with the human eyes and what one can see through spiritual eyes. There is a great difference.

"What are they going to do?" Kim asked.

"They're going to break into my van and everyone else's cars in the neighborhood. They'll steal everything of any value and destroy everything else!"

"What? That's crazy! How do you know that?" Kim said as she started to get up.

I grabbed her hand, and she got back down on her knees next to me.

"Watch for yourself!"

As Kim continued watching, I asked if she would do exactly what I told her to, when I told her to, and she agreed.

"Okay then, not another word. Just watch and listen to me."

I got up off my knees and parted the blinds a bit higher, making sure I could reach the light switch.

"Okay" she sighed. "Oh, my God. Lisa, they're going for your van!"

I watched patiently as one took up position behind the van and the other moved in to get a look in the driver's side window.

I flipped on the garage door spotlight to make them think they'd triggered a motion detector. Startled, they began to walk down the dark street as fast as they could without looking obvious. I counted to six and then switched the light off.

Little did they know, they'd lost the game this evening before they had even started to play. It was now only a matter of time before all the pieces were moved into place and the board swept clean.

"I'll be right back. Stay here, Kim. I mean it!"

"Be careful, Lisa."

Her warning reminded me of the many times my mother would say, "Lisa, be careful!" I'd just smile and assure her, too.

Stepping out the front door, I began to assess the situation. In a matter of seconds, I had a plan. Running toward the truck as fast as I could, I dodged the streetlights and stayed in the shadows. Nearing the truck, I took down the tag number, make and model. There was a third man who'd stayed behind to watch the truck, but he was definitely not a good watch dog!

Next, I set out to find what the others were up to.

Disappearing in the darkness, I made a right behind the truck, then another right at the corner. I peeked over a large bush at the side of the corner house and could plainly see one of them inside a big red work truck parked only two houses down from my van. The other guy was looking in the windows of a car parked in the driveway.

Quickly, I made my way back to the house. I gave Kim the signal to call 911 and handed her the license plate information. Finally, I could sit down and catch my breath.

"Lisa, dispatch wants to talk to you," Kim said as she handed me the phone.

"Is this Lisa Everly?" the dispatcher said.

"Yes, it is. I have the information you need on the car vandals. They're two houses down." I guess she recognized me because dispatch and I had talked so many times about hospital security matters.

I provided the dispatcher with the rest of the information she needed. Telling me that one unit was in the neighborhood and another was close by, she asked which direction the first patrol car should approach the red work truck from.

After hanging up the phone, I went back out to the driveway and watched as the two men rummaged through the work truck. Hiding behind Kim's truck, I could see the head of one man bobbing up and down as he ransacked the interior of the truck. The first patrol car silently rolled onto the dark street behind them.

By the time the overheads came on, there was little time for either of the men to put up much of a fight, and they were handcuffed rather quickly. The second patrol car rolled up behind their truck still sitting in the dark on Colton. The officer opened the door and yanked the third man out from his hiding place behind the seat.

"For a moment, it looked like a terrier dragging a rabbit out of its hole!" I say with a chuckle to Janie, who is still hanging on every word. "You should have seen it, sis. I thought that cop was going to pull the guy's pants right off him!"

Janie laughs.

I know my sister, and she has a colorful visual on that one.

"I wonder if those were the same guys who broke into my truck a few weeks after I moved into this neighborhood." I smile to myself and think how funny things sometimes work out.

"Anyway, they caught them red-handed, hauled them to jail and the theft stopped. Who knows how many others they named, as well?"

I tell Janie how the officer came back to the house a little later to talk to me, thanking me for what I'd done and asking if I wanted it known that I was the one who'd stopped them. I said that wasn't necessary. Shaking my hand as he left, he said, "Good work." I smiled and said, "Thanks, officer."

L. Robinson Garden

Dasies

17 Evil Spirit Experience

Finishing the story, I let my last words hang in the darkness. I wonder what part of the story Janie will want to ask me about. Before the silence is broken, Terry stumbles through the living room in the dark, still reeling from her hangover. Unable to see Janie and I lying on the floor, she clips my leg and lands right on top of us.

"Hey! What the heck are you guys doing lying in the middle of the floor?"

"Lisa's telling me about her stopping a crime spree," Janie says. Not able to resist a dig, she adds, "At least we're not down here passed out!"

Terry picks herself up, laughs and says, "Yeah. Sorry about that, guys. It's been a rough week."
"You want to sit in on some more of Lisa's 'ghost stories'?"

"Sure," Terry says as she returns with a glass of water and sits down on the couch. "I've heard some of her stories, and I particularly love the one about when she rebuilt the engine in her truck when she was only seventeen."

"I already know that story," Janie says like it's no big deal. "Have you heard about the evil spirit at the church and the time my cousin Jana and I saw it standing right behind Lisa years ago? It was the same one as at the church!"

"I don't usually tell people those stories, Janie," I say.

"Why? You should! They are very important, and people should hear about them."

"Evil spirits?" Terry asks.

"Has Lisa told you anything about her life? She's very interesting, and all her stories are true. Everyone knows that!" Janie says as if she were sticking up for me on the playground.

"Okay then. I would love to hear one."

"Wouldn't you guys rather play Scrabble or something?" I ask, of course they don't, so I reluctantly agree, and we all settle back down on the floor with the candles flickering around us. Goose bumps rise on my arms and a cold shiver runs down my spine as the experience comes rushing back into my mind.

I was fourteen, and until that day I had never truly seen the face of evil. I knew evil existed and had seen it in the face of the man who raped me, but it wasn't until that day that I realized evil could enter our world in its own recognizable physical form.

I had overheard Mom and Dad talking about how they never had a vacation by themselves. Dad told mom how much he wanted to go to the coast for a few days.

Mom talked to Aunt Paula about her and Uncle John watching us for a few days so they could get away. They agreed, so Mom and Dad dropped us off that weekend at their home in Norwalk.

My aunt and uncle worked for a church, and their home was on the property. Uncle John took care of the grounds, worked on the busses, managed the bus ministry and was occasionally called to preach. Aunt Paula taught Sunday school, cleaned the church on weekends and raised their two sons, Luke and Mark.

The first day we were there, my aunt was cleaning the church with a couple of other ladies from the congregation. She said I could join her and the other ladies if I wanted to. Everyone would be up front in the main building cleaning for the next hour while uncle John was studying in the pastor's office if we needed anything.

The rest of the kids were watching TV and I was lying on the couch. About thirty minutes passed, and I got bored and decided to go help clean. Telling the other kids where I was going, I shut the door behind me and headed for the church. As I walked past the busses, all lined up and ready to go the next morning, I stopped and looked around because I had the feeling that someone was watching me.

Something didn't seem right, and suddenly chills ran down my arms and back. The heavy gray feeling blanketed me, awakening my spiritual senses. My every sense was heightened to the extreme, and I was acutely aware of even the most obscure details I would normally dismiss.

Continuing down the driveway toward the Sunday school classrooms, the feeling got heavier. I wasn't sure what was going on, but I knew something wasn't right. Reaching the front door of the church, I let out a breath of relief as I saw my aunt gathering her supplies to move on to the next room. She suggested that I stay behind in the room they'd just cleaned to do the final vacuuming. I agreed and the ladies moved on to the building next door.

When I was done, I rolled up the cord and put the vacuum away. I went next door to find my aunt and tell her I was finished. Not able to find her, I decided to walk back to the house and resume my position on the couch. Outside, I reached the front of the Sunday school building and stopped dead in my tracks. The heavy gray feeling had returned and was so intense it was impossible to take another step.

This time, I knew for sure that something was watching me. As I turned around, I saw what it was. I couldn't believe what my eyes were seeing.

There it was, floating above the grass in front of the two-story building. I had never seen anything so evil.

It was a transparent gray, and a long, dark robe hung over its body in thick folds, covering its arms down to its long, bony hands. The hood of the robe seemed to rest atop a faceless black abyss, which held two fire-red eyes that never blinked. They never took their gaze off me as they seemingly tried to burn into my soul.

I began to pray to God for protection. "Our Father, who art in heaven…"

It was about twenty feet in front of me, and neither one of us was moving. We were frozen in place, each of us undecided about what move to make next. I felt as if I were in some kind of stand off. But then it raised its arm.

"What do you want?" I demanded.

Like a willow in the breeze, its shrouded arm made a smooth, welcoming gesture. "Come to me," it motioned. Forward and back, its hand circled as it tried to lure me closer. I could feel it pulling at my mind, but my strength and faith were strong. My feet remained firmly planted.

Then, through all the thoughts in my head, I heard my six-year-old cousin, Luke, call out to me from the other end of the parking lot.

"Wun, Weesa! It's the Devil!" he screamed.

His cries pulled me out of the trance I'd fallen into, and for a moment I took my attention off the spirit and focused on Luke's words. He was standing in front of the line of busses, pleading with me to run for my life. Still, I couldn't move. When I looked back, the spirit had advance four feet in my direction.

Refocused, I continued reciting the Lord's Prayer, and the spirit stayed where it was. It had gotten one opportunity, but I was going to make sure it didn't get another.

We were once again at a stand still when I noticed a dog peeking its head out from the breezeway that ran between the Sunday school building and the nursery. It crouched low to the ground and very carefully peered around the corner. Its movements were very deliberate and for a few moments it stared straight at me, motionless, from about forty feet away.

As each of them stared at me, there seemed to be a kind of collaboration between them, and when the dog disappeared I knew I was in terrible danger. It was now two against one, and I knew the odds were no longer in my favor. Now was the time to run!

I finished the last line of the prayer in my head. I wasn't taking any chances so I turned and ran toward Luke as fast as I could. We met in the middle of the driveway and together ran back to my aunt's house. I don't remember if my feet even touched the ground because it felt like the angel had given me wings I never looked back to see if the spirit or dog were coming after me.

Bursting through the front door, Luke and I tried to catch our breath to tell Aunt Paula what we'd seen. I hardly believed it myself, so how was I going to convince anyone else? But when Aunt Paula saw my face, I had the feeling she already knew what had happened.

"Lisa! What's the matter? Do you want me to call uncle John?"

"Yes," I answered as I gasped for a breath of air.

She picked up the phone and rang the church office.

"John, come right away. It's Lisa. I believe she saw something and it may have to do with…well, you know."

She slowly hung up the phone and stared into space for a moment. I could tell she was in a bit of shock. My uncle had told her something just then on the phone. I didn't know what he said, but it seemed to distract her even more.

"Lisa, Uncle John will be here. Just give him a little time. He's…in the middle of something important right now."

While we waited, Aunt Paula questioned me about what it looked like and what it wanted, and I explained it step-by-step until my uncle arrived.

After hearing an overview, John asked me to come with him into the den. Seating himself in an armchair, he motioned for me to sit on the couch. He slid his chair closer and rested his elbows on his knees so he could look me in the face and talk to me like an adult.

He explained to me that everyone at the church had been working very hard and because of that, many people's lives were changing. The congregation had grown from one hundred and fifty to two thousand in a very short time, and when there are souls being saved the devil will begin lurking around, looking for a way to destroy it.

I told him I understood, answered the rest of his questions and made an agreement with him that this would be kept quiet for fear it would scare off new members. If this got out, it could hurt more than help. Most people wouldn't recognize the demon's presence as an indicator of God's success, but rather of his failure or even worse, his absence. I understood the importance of the preservation of faith, so I knew this had to be kept secret.

For years, I never told a soul. Then one day, years later when I was much older, my uncle and I had another talk about what actually happened that day.

He told me that while I was facing the evil spirit, he was visited in his office by an angel of God, who explained everything to him. He said the angel knew that I would face the demon and pass unharmed, and it also told him how to explain it to me so I'd understand the reason for its appearance.

Prior to that day, the local dog catcher, police and several others related stories of the evil spirit collaborating with the dog, even entering the dog, in order to attack people. After a lengthy pursuit, the animal was finally captured, only to break free and disappear. The dog catcher claimed it was smarter and stronger than any dog he had ever seen. Since its escape, It hadn't been seen again until my experience with it that day. After that it disappeared for good.

The evil spirit never appeared to anyone at the church again. And, even though it hasn't directly appeared to me again either, those in my presence have reported they've seen it approaching me from behind.

A little gasp of astonishment breaks the silence, and I suddenly remember I have an audience. That's a hard story to tell, partly because it's so personally powerful and partly because it's so unbelievable in some people's minds. The worst that may happen is Terry will start leaving lights on, worried that the evil spirit may come looking for me and she'll get caught in the crossfire.

Right away, the questions start. "Weren't you scared to death? I think I would have died of a heart attack right on the spot!" Janie says.

"This thing tried to make you come to it? Wow! What was going through your mind?" Terry adds.

"Well, actually, I was thinking, 'Yeah, right. Like I'm just going to walk over there to you because you're waving that pointy little finger at me!'"

Janie lets out a roar of laughter. It's good to see the seriousness lifting so we can all go back to having a good time. There's one point Terry's waiting to make, and it's a factor I've put some thought into over the years, too.

"So, this evil spirit wore a dark, flowing robe with a hood, and it had red eyes, skeleton hands and no face? Kind of sounds like something Hollywood invented," she says in a way that isn't accusing but indicates she still has some doubt about its authenticity.

"I agree. That's one of the first things I thought, too. I guess it makes sense, because I've been in the presence of angels in white robes. But who would have thought that an actual evil spirit or angel would look like its portrayal in the movies? Maybe it means the images we use to represent the grim reaper, demons and evil spirits actually came down through human history because of actual sightings. Maybe it means that we have a built-in knowledge of the spiritual realms and we don't consciously realize it?

Terry's next question is one I've wondered all my life. "Why have all these things happened to you?"

I sit deep in thought for a few moments before answering.

The only answer I have been able to give myself is the same answer I've been giving others all my life, that as far back as I can remember I have always felt like part of a bigger picture.

"It hasn't been easy and on top of that, I have to deal with you two!" I say jokingly as I give Janie a little nudge.

She starts to laugh and push back while Terry tries to look stern and says, "What about us having to deal with you, huh?"

Terry joins in the fray, and finally we're all lying on the floor trying to catch our breath.

"So, you guys ready to go to sleep?" I ask.

"No! I want to tell the story of when I saw the evil spirit sneaking up behind you at Sissy's house. That was so scary! I will never forget it as long as I live, and Sissy won't either," Janie says, pleading with us to say up a bit longer.

"Alright, sis. Go ahead," I say, and we all settle back down on our pillows.

As Janie starts telling the story, I find myself reliving it through her voice. Not a detail is changed as she relates it just as I remember it happening.

I must have been about twenty-two years old, which would have made Janie about eight. We were at my uncle's house in Tahlequah, Oklahoma, visiting with him, his wife and their daughter, Jana, who everyone called Sissy. She was Janie's age. The adults had left me at the house to watch the kids while they went out for a bit. I settled down in a big armchair to watch television while Janie and Sissy sat on the floor between the couch and the coffee table, playing with their toys.

There was a short entryway between the living room and the front door, which had a six-inch-by-eight-inch glass window, allowing a person to see who was standing on the stoop. While the chair I was sitting in was backed up to the wall just to the right of the entry, the girls were playing in direct line to the front door. I couldn't see the door from where I was sitting, so their faces and reactions were all I saw.

I had started to get that gray feeling and was beginning to feel uncomfortable and fidget in my chair. Their talking got too loud, and I told them to be quiet so I could watch TV. Actually, I needed them to be quiet so I could concentrate on the source of my growing restlessness.

"I remember that I started to ask you a question," Janie says, "when I saw something in the little window on the door.

All of a sudden the bright sunlight shining through the little window was replaced by darkness, like night had suddenly come in the middle of the day. And then, in the center of the black window, I saw two red, fiery eyes.

I don't think I even finished the question I was asking you when I saw those eyes. It was like I was frozen. I couldn't take my eyes off them."

Indeed, she had stopped in mid-sentence. I remember she had a complete look of fear and surprise on her face. Sissy was still playing with her toys until she looked up to see what Janie was staring at. And then the blood drained from her face, as well.

"And then this thing just *flowed* through the door!" Janie says, waving her hands. "Little by little, it just stepped or floated or whatever into the room."

I remember her saying, "Lisa! Oh my God, Lisa! What is it?" Every hair on my body was standing straight up and a cold chill was running down my back. I knew what it was.

"It was the most terrifying thing I've ever seen," Janie says. "You know what it felt like? It was like one of those nightmares you have as a kid, where you're so scared that you can't run and you can't yell. You're just frozen in your dream, screaming in your head, trying to make your legs move but they won't."

I cringe, thinking of that comparison. That's exactly what it felt like.

"It just hovered inside the doorway for a moment and then slowly started to come toward us. That was when you got up from the chair."

I remember that I was praying the entire time, and not once did I turn around and look at what Janie was pointing at. Coming around behind them, I placed my left hand on Janie and my right hand on Sissy. I calmly turned and lifted my eyes, finally ready to face it again after all those years.

"And then it just disappeared!" Janie says. "It just vanished into thin air."

She was right. It vanished before I ever set eyes on it, but I didn't need to see it to know it was there.

I held the frightened girls and told them everything would be okay. I asked them to tell me what they'd seen, and they described exactly what I'd seen that day at the church: a large, transparent entity draped in a heavy robe, whose face held nothing more than a black emptiness with mesmerizing eyes of fire. I think Sissy described it as a "mean ghost."

"I will never forget what I saw that day as long as I live," Janie said as she expelled a long-held breath.

"Wow!" Terry yells. "These stories are amazing. How come you haven't written a book yet?"

"Good question. I haven't yet, but I will! For now, though, I am going to bed. You two exhaust me."

"Can I sleep in your room, Lisa?" Janie laughs as she looks over at Terry, who is still deep in thought.

"NO! Good night, ladies."

We put the pillows back on the couch and our tea cups in the sink. And one by one, we gather our things and head off to our rooms. I'm so tired, I barely make it under the sheets before I'm asleep.

18   Jill-of-all-Trades

The sun is shining through my bedroom window, and the smell of bacon cooking wakes me up from a wonderful dream. I hate it when that happens! Closing my eyes, I try to fall asleep again. I was on stage with my keyboard, rockin' out as hard as I could. Lights and smoke filled the stadium, and the crowd was going wild and chanting, "Lisa! Lisa!" I can see it all so clearly in my mind, but I know I'm simply lying in bed grasping at images of how I wish my life had turned out. It's time to get up and go to work.

Pulling on a pair of sweats and a T-shirt, I make my way into the kitchen. Janie's sitting at the kitchen table with the entire morning paper spread out before her. The ads and sections she isn't interested in have been exiled under her chair, and a row of colored highlighters lay at the ready along the top of the help wanted section. She looks like a woman on a mission.

"Trying to find a job? Any good prospects?" I ask.

"Oh, there's a few. Problem is, I'm not really sure what I want to do, or even what some of these jobs are," She says with a sigh of discouragement and sits back in her chair.

I give her a pat on the back and a smile and tell her not to give up. "You'll find something you like."

"You've done just about everything there is to do, Lisa. What did you like best? Or better question, what do you think I'd like the best?" she says with a laugh because she knows I've never been shy about telling my family what I think they should be doing. I'll tell her stories about what I've done and what I've found rewarding in each career. Somewhere along the way, maybe she'll recognize something that feels right for her.

As I sip my tea, I recall the happiest job I ever had. I was probably about twelve years old, and I remember the voices calling out, "Hey, Blondie. How much for this?"

I learned to be resourceful from my parents at an early age. Often we were financially poor, but our house didn't reflect it. Mom and Dad would find furniture at sales or take items that were given to them and fix them up to look brand new. By the time I was ten I knew how to make one good thing out of three broken ones and how to paint and patch just about anything. Dad and I would dumpster dive or scavenge through the landfill and Mom and I would visit every garage sale, then off we'd go to the swap meet. My grandfather always said, "If you have something to sell, you'll never go hungry," and we never did.

Most importantly, I learned how to sell what we'd fixed. Whether it was a bicycle or a lemon squeezer, I could convince someone to buy it, even if they didn't know they needed it. We never cheated anyone or sold them something we knew didn't work. If a customer came back because what they bought didn't work, we always gave them their money back. That was my mother's motto, and because of that we sold more than anyone else.

Typically, we'd pack the truck and leave for the swap meet at about three o'clock in the morning. Driving down into LA, we'd get in line at the Paramount Swap Meet and wait for the gates to open, only to have other sellers and some buyers come down the line looking for a good buy. Some days we would sell the majority of our things before we even got through the gates, but on others we'd have enough left to go inside and set up our booth.

I would carefully set out each item, set up the tables and put out the glass-topped jewelry cases. I had a strategy behind the placement of every item, and I would re-strategize and move the items around throughout the day.

"Never let your booth picked over, and when something sells put something back in its place. No empty holes," my mother would say.

Once Mom saw I had everything under control, she'd head off to check the other booths for unrecognized values. While other sellers simply sat on their tailgates waiting for people to ask them questions, I was more like a sideshow barker, greeting every passerby and enticing them to stop and take a look at what we had. I'd tell them how pretty it would be in their home or how much easier it would make their life if they bought it. When they asked how much it cost, I'd pause for a moment like I had to think about it. Starting with an amount a little higher than I expected, we'd barter until the price was where I wanted it and the customer felt like they'd gotten a deal. Everyone walked away happy.

The price wasn't the same for every customer. I always had charity for the poor and higher prices for the rich, who'd looked down their noses at me and offer little for what they called "old junk."

I remember how rewarding it was to see a mother walk by with two or three little girls. She would ask, 'Do you have any shoes today?" and I would tell her, "Sorry. Not today," and as they would start to walk away, the youngest would catch sight of the bike I'd just finished repairing.

Bright and shiny with fresh paint and sparkling tassels from the handlebars, it would be positioned in the front row, within easy reach of the intended customer.

"Mommy, look. A bike!" she'd say, pulling her mother toward it.

"Not today. We don't have enough money."

"But Mommy, it's so pretty! Please?"

I knew that feeling and recognized the face of a child caught between the excitement of a simple joy and the disappointment of something there was never enough extra money for.

It would break my heart to see the mother gently trying to pry the child's fingers from the handlebars with promises of "maybe later."

"She can sit on it for a moment, can't she?" I'd say before the mother had to carry the child away in tears.

Getting down on one knee, I'd say, "Don't you look pretty on that beautiful blue bike?"

She would smile and run her fingers through the tassels. When I'd look up, the mother would be smiling, too, but holding back the tears of knowing she would have to pull the child away in a moment.

"I think you should have this beautiful bike, don't you?"

Looking up at the mother, I'd say, "Why don't you take it—my gift to you."

When Mom returned, she'd look over the booth and ask me what I'd gotten for each item. When she would get around to the bicycle, I'd say, "I gave it away....but the boat motor you wanted twenty dollars for I sold to a rich man for forty. He still got a good deal. It ran like a charm."

Mom would just smile and say, "Well, looks like we're going to have a really good day. Keep it up, and I'll be back in a while."

As the day went by, there would be a steady stream of customers and I would greet each in their own language. I knew just enough Spanish and Japanese to say hello, barter back and forth and then close the sale. I knew "hello," "yes," "no," "very best," "works well," "thank you", and of course, all the prices.

There were a few odd phrases I needed to know, like "Miguel, you know I can't marry you." Miguel would come by almost every week and say to my mother, "You know, I'm going to marry your daughter someday!" She'd just smile and talk him into buying something instead.

When four o'clock rolled around, we'd start packing up our remaining items as the last few stragglers came around to talk us down to half price. Sometimes I'd take them up on their offer if it was a heavy item Mom was dreading putting back in the truck.

Once everything was sold or reloaded back into the truck, Mom and I would pull out the dustpan and broom and sweep our space clean. Not a shred of packing paper or fallen gum wrapper from a shopper's pocket left behind. While other booths were left with bags, bottles and paper cups, ours was always spotless. "Never leave a mess for others to pick up," my mother would always say—and we never did.

"You know, Janie, you could be like Mom and go to garage sales and flea markets. I loved doing that as a kid.

But you probably want something that's a little more reliable don't you? It's not easy working for yourself, and you have to be really self-motivated. Let's think about nine-to-five type stuff."

Janie is interested in all the jobs I've done, so I try my best to remember them all. I take a sip of tea and begin listing them off.

> auto repossessor
> auto sales
> business owner
>> (auto detailing)
>> (commercial cleaning co.)
>> (senior care facility)
>> (window tinting)
> camp counselor
> city bus driver
> class A long-haul truck driver and instructor
> collection agent
> construction worker
> factory worker
>> (auto-wheel manufacturing)
>> (clothing production)
>> (hat designer)
>> (nursery worker)
>> (plastics manufacturing)
>> (soup canning)
> jewelry sales
> landscaper
> mini-mart clerk
> nurses' assistant
> nurses' registry manager
> office secretary

painter
photographer
property maintenance
remodeler
restaurant manager
    (BBQ)
    (Mexican)
    (pizza)
security officer
    (hospitals, banks, airports and railroads)
    (housing projects, movie sets and concerts)
Last, but probably not least, window washer.

"Whew! I think that just about covers it. I'm sure I've for-gotten a few, but that's it for the most part. How did I do?"

"What about x, y and z?" she asks sarcastically.

"I still have x-ray technician, yodeler and zebra trainer on my to-do list." I say trying to seem serious. "Don't go asking me to recite the hundred-plus places I've lived. I couldn't do that. Probably because I don't want to remember everything that went along with moving that much."

Janie can see the pain in my eyes and doesn't ask.

"That's quite a list you've got there! Which one do you think I should try?"

As much as she would love for me to just tell her how to fix her life, I'm not going to do that. I can tell her what I found rewarding about certain jobs, or what problems I had, but the rest is up to her to figure out.

Janie taps her pen on the paper as I tell her some of the lessons I've learned along the way. I explained that I learned to be resourceful and outgoing from selling repaired items we'd found at the dump or garage sales and how this also taught me kindness, fairness, responsibility and math, as well as communicating with various cultures.

I learned about power through authority with respect and how to gain people's cooperation without resorting to physical restraint, threats or violence while I worked as a security guard in the projects.

While working in hospice and senior care, I learned about the power of hope and the devastation of the spirit when its lost. I sat with the dying, comforted the living and recognized the importance of quality in every stage of life.

Driving an eighteen-wheeler taught me respect for nature and self-reliance when I brought a loaded rig through an "impassable" mountain blizzard with a terrified trainee in the passenger seat. It also gave me the opportunity to listen to and advise those who found comfort in telling me about their lives while we drove along the endless stretches of highway.

Through the years I've saved lives, changed lives, stopped crimes and helped others start their own businesses. At the same time, I have come close to death several times, been harassed at work, gang raped, shot at and set up. More than once, I reached the top and walked away.

I stop for a moment to let Janie think about what I've said, and I ask myself, "What will I tell her was the best job I've ever had?" It certainly wasn't the one that paid the most. In fact, the best "job" I've ever had has been helping others spiritually—and I have never charged a cent for it.

The rewards have been boundless. I have helped people put their lives back on track, including teens and adults considering suicide. When I've shown people they can make better choices and truly have power in their lives, they regain a sense of directing their own destiny, instead of being helplessly controlled by everything around them.

And in doing so, they regain their spirit, as well.

It amazes me when people start telling me their life story in passing. I can be standing in the grocery store line or fixing someone's drain and they will start telling me about their life's deepest pain. Often, they are things most of us would find difficult to tell our closest friends. I feel that God sees them cross my path and creates a moment of healing—made through Spirit without judgment.

"Lisa, you certainly are a Jill-of-all-trades," Janie says as she sets the list aside. "But really. Tell me what you see me doing!"

"I think you need to ask yourself that," I say with a hint of big-sister scolding.

I put my hand on her shoulder and tell her, "Look at what you have done. Do you want to continue in that direction? Or, if there is something you've always wanted to do, to ask yourself how you can start working toward it. You might need to volunteer or take a class first."

Suddenly, I feel as if I'm back in my old camp counselor job. But now I'm giving advice on something more life-changing than how to treat mosquito bites or row a canoe in a straight line. It's similar to the discussion on how to not get lost in the woods. Like any big sister, I want to see my little sister find her way in this world.

"But if you really don't have an idea, then perhaps you need to find out who *you* are and what you really want. Make a list of what you like, what you find rewarding and even what nobody could pay you enough to do."

"Yeah, like picking up doggie doo, or climbing down into one of those little holes under the street or having to be to work before eight o'clock in the morning!" Janie says excitedly, like she was finally able to answer one of my questions correctly.

"At least she knows what she doesn't want to do!" I think to myself. "That's a start."

"Every job has its ups and downs, and even the most seemingly boring job may have remarkable moments if you leave yourself open to them."

"But what do you…?" Janie says, still unaware that I'm not going to answer the question for her.

"You know, something extraordinary happened to me one night when I was on duty. I thought it was the most boring job I'd ever had. That night gave me one of my most memorable and powerful experiences."

Janie pours another cup of tea and yells out to Terry, "Lisa's going to tell us another story. You better get in here."

A few minutes later, Terry stumbles out of the bathroom and grabs her favorite cup out of the dishwasher. "I wouldn't miss it for the world. What's the topic this morning?"

I begin to laugh because as I look around the table, I think, "Here we sit, a forty-one-year-old, a thirty-five-year-old and a thirty-two-year-old, sipping tea and reminiscing about our pasts like it was centuries ago."

I look at Janie and Terry and wonder where they'll be ten years from now. Will Janie stay off drugs? Will Terry stay sober and quit coming to the breakfast table topless?

As they sit quietly, waiting for me to begin the story, I realize how important the stories from my life have been to them and how they have helped them think differently and make better choices. Somewhere in the back of my mind, I am actually starting to feel good about my past. What I've experienced has allowed me to help others, and this has been a wonderful healing tool for myself at the same time. I am beginning to feel very blessed.

Yard Sale Prices

© Lisa L. Everly 2006

Flower Power (cropped)

19

Blue Angel

"So what about the story, Lisa?" Janie yells after slinging her burnt toast into the kitchen sink.

Terry begins to laugh and adds, "Let's face it. You definitely shouldn't apply for a cook's position!"

I have to laugh out loud, too.

"Oh, mind your own affairs, Terry. You couldn't fight your way out of a paper bag without those Coke-bottle glasses!" Janie snickers.

"Well, at least…"

"Okay, ladies. Here's the story. Have I ever told you the one about the blue angel that appeared on my night watch out in the desert?"

Terry shakes her head "no."

"I'd been working for a woman who owned and operated a security business in Hesperia, California. I worked days, weekends, swing and nights. It wasn't too boring because each assignment was a little different from the last. One week, I'd be working in a housing project or a bank, and the next I might be doing security at a local event, movie set or TV commercial site. All in all, it was a pretty good job. It just wasn't what I really wanted to be doing with my life."

On that particular day, I was supposed to work at a housing project but my schedule got changed at the last minute. Instead I was being sent to the dry riverbed outside Victorville where a crew was shooting a furniture commercial in the middle of the desert. It would be hot during the day and cold at night, without facilities for miles, and three long nights...alone. That made me a little nervous, but I headed home to pack what I'd need for the assignment.

Working nights meant a whole different setup on my duty belt. Along with my non-lethal deterrent and cell phone, I added a larger flashlight, a ten-in-one tool kit and two sets of cuffs. I also put a second set of batteries in my bag along with a pair of blue jeans, a T-shirt, socks and a change of underwear.

As I packed extra underwear I remembered mom telling us that we should always be wearing clean underwear in case we got into an accident and had to be taken to the hospital. Odd what parents think is vitally important enough to drill into our psyches for the rest of our lives. I wasn't planning on getting hurt, but I figured it wouldn't be a bad idea.

I threw my lightweight jacket over my shoulder, wrapped my heavy coat around my overnight bag and finished packing an ice chest full of bottled water, sodas, BBQ sandwiches and homemade chocolate chip cookies. The cookies reminded me of Mom, too. She would always bake me something special to make me feel better if I was a little apprehensive about something.

It was ten o'clock at night and I was excited. At the same time, I was a little worried, because the map and directions I'd been given at the office were not that good, and I hadn't been to the riverbeds before. It took me a while, but I made it without any problems. When I arrived some of the setup crew was still there, and they directed me to the person in charge. His name was Mark.

Mark was a nice guy. He instructed me on the setup and showed me around the set.

"You know you'll be out here in the pitch-black darkness once I shut down the generator, don't you?" he asked.

"No, I didn't. But I'm okay with that. I'm used to working in the dark," I assured him.

"You're not afraid to be out here by yourself?" he asked.

"No. I'm never alone."

He smiled and then pointed out the main tent. "That one has all the expensive equipment in it, so patrol it the most."

"I sure will. It'll all be here safe and sound in the morning," I assured him.

"I can tell you've done this before, Lisa," he said, smiling. "I'm going to send the other two home, and then before I leave I'll shut off the power. I'll warn you before I do."

After a few minutes, I heard Mark yell, "All power off!" and I found myself standing in pitch-black darkness. I couldn't even see my hand in front of my face. My stomach twitched a bit with discomfort.

"I'm leaving, Lisa," he yelled from behind the main tent.

I watched his headlights fade into the darkness, then looked around and realized it was much darker than I thought it would be. There was no moon that night, and although I tried to focus my eyes enough to see at least an outline of the tents, it was no use.

Pausing outside the main tent, I listened. There were

no sounds other than the distant conversation of coyotes making their way through the desert. I don't remember what felt worse: the vulnerability, the loneliness or the boredom. Through the night, I found myself feeling a little of each. Saying a prayer, I convinced myself that I was safe and that the rest of the night would go by quickly...I hoped.

The hot, dry night was becoming a lot cooler as early morning arrived, and I found myself reaching for my coat. My watch said 2:20 a.m. as I leaned up against my car and thought about eating my lunch a little early. I decided to wait until later, but I did eat my chocolate chip cookies.

As I continued my rounds I began thinking to myself, "Why am I doing this? Why have I chosen this line of work? This is the most boring and tiring work I have ever done." It was the closest thing to my dream job I could do at the time. Not having attended college, it didn't seem likely that I would ever become a motorcycle cop. I was feeling a bit hopeless and figured this was the only work I would be able to get.

I began to think about my life and why things turned out the way they did. I felt left behind and abandoned, and I didn't feel like I was doing what I was here to do. The tears came streaming from my eyes. I had so many dreams when I was younger, but the more bad things happened to me the less I felt like I had what it would take to reach those aspirations. I couldn't go back and change the past, and I was beginning to feel like I couldn't go forward either.

I must have thought about my life for quite a while because through my contemplation I noticed the morning light starting to break over the mountain. Soon, the crew began to arrive and I gave Mark an update on the evening. "It was a very quiet night," I told him.

He thanked me and told me to have a great day—or in my case a great night—and that he'd see me later for my second shift. Packing my things into the car, I followed the tire tracks in the sand all the way back to the highway and made it home without trouble.

The second night was a little different. I started into the desert at about 10:20 p.m. No lights directed me to the tents; it appeared that everyone had already left.

Driving slowly I followed the heavy traffic lines in the sand for about an hour and finally found the site. It was strange having to search for it and even stranger that they left the place unattended with no one waiting for me. Someone could have arrived before I showed up and hid in one of the tents.

I pulled my car up to the main tent and turned on my high beams, unzipped the front and peeked inside. Wow! It was beautiful in there. It looked like a kitchen that could have come straight out of a magazine. For a moment I forgot I was looking for an intruder, but I snapped out of it and zipped the tent back up.

As I continued to patrol the site, I realized there were hundreds of thousands of dollars in furnishings, props, decorations, lights, camera setups and small stages built into different settings. My curiosity was growing more intense, and I couldn't wait to peek in the other tents to see what treasures I might find.

I returned to my car, turned off the lights, grabbed my flashlight and began my perimeter patrol on foot. The next tent looked like it had been setup for the crew. It had couches, cots and tables covered with wrapped-up food. Lots of ice chests filled with drinks and water bottles were sitting around.

Grabbing a handful of grapes, I sat down on a beautiful couch that was in the corner on a large piece of carpet. I wondered what it would be like to work as a film director and have a crew bring my artistic vision to life. I was sure I could get used to something like that as I tested the grapes to make sure they were good.

The crew's tent was comfortable but boring, and I made my way back to the tent where the stages were set up and began to perform my own furniture commercial. Just as I was reciting my made-up lines about quality and afford-ability, I quickly jumped off the stage when I heard something outside.

Grabbing my flashlight from my duty belt, I squatted down and listened quietly in the darkness. I shifted into what I call my security mode, where I use all my senses to the best of their ability.

Not knowing what might be out there, I yelled, "Hey guys! Did you hear that?" as I began rumbling boxes and making the sounds of many people getting up to check on the situation. Then the noise stopped.

I quickly illuminated the tent and continued making loud noises when my flashlight revealed a fleeing coyote who had made off with my sack lunch while I was busy playing movie star. I arrived at the scene, and there wasn't one crumb left. All I could think was, "That's one lucky coyote to get Mom's famous barbecue for dinner!"

I closed the tent, walked over and sat down on the hood of my car. My watch read 2:57 a.m. and there was nothing but darkness, silence and hours left to check and recheck the tents. My stomach grumbled. The next four hours were going to seem like an eternity.

Looking up at the stars, I quietly said a prayer. As I

looked back down from the starry sky, there was a small, blue ball of light hovering over the riverbed. It seemed far away, but as I focused on it I realized it was slowly, coming closer, getting lower and heading toward me.

At first I thought it might be a plane, but that didn't seem quite right. Then I thought it might be a distraction that would allow something else to come upon me. It wouldn't have been the first time.

A fearfulness began to sweep over me, and I felt the safest place was in my car. I quickly climbed in, locked the doors and started the engine in case I had to make a run for it. When I looked again, I could tell it had advanced a little further. I stared intensely to see what it was. As I followed it, I also watched my rearview mirror to make sure there was nothing approaching behind me. My entire body shook, and every breath I took seemed to echo through me. If only I knew what I was facing, then I could handle the situation.

As I recited the Lord's Prayer, the blue ball of light began to take on a shape. At first, it appeared to be the outline of someone in a long, flowing robe. Then it began to reveal broad, folded wings. They slowly opened, spreading wide above the angel's shoulders forming a spectacular presence that was over thirty feet high. This was unlike any angel I'd been in the presence of before.

The blue was breathtaking, vibrant and alive, unlike any color I had ever seen. It was like a neon royal blue with a bright white light shining through it. The white light created a silhouette as it cast a shadow along the riverbed in front of it.

As I realized what this presence was, my fear left. I unlocked the door, got out and calmly stood in front of my

car, waiting for what would happen next. As I stood mes-
merized by its beauty, the desert and the tents disappeared.
My spirit was filled with a familiar, overwhelming peace.

In the past, angels had come to save me. Was I in danger? Was it my spirit that was in danger? God knew how
troubled and depressed I had become. I hoped this time
there would be some answers to my questions.

From somewhere deep in my mind, the angel told
me not to be afraid and that the work I'd done had not
gone unnoticed. All the different jobs I'd done were not
just to survive. They were important because God needed
me there. Each time, in some way, my presence had been
important to someone else's journey.

Tears ran down my face when the blue angel told me
that no matter where I was, or where I went, God would
always watch over me and that I should not be afraid but
happy, because my treasures are not of this world.

Terry's sobbing pulls me from my memories and back
to the present. She takes off her glasses to wipe her eyes
as Janie lays her head on my shoulder. I think about how
selfish I've been to doubt myself through the years, and in
my mind I ask God to forgive me.

What I realize now by remembering the angel's words
is that I'm helping my friends and family by telling them
my experiences. When I pretend none of those things
happened because I'm afraid of what others may say or
think, I'm doing the wrong thing. I'm not afraid anymore.
All anyone can do is call me crazy. Big deal! I am not trying to convince anyone of anything, I'm simply telling my
story and hoping it might help others.

Terry and Janie throw their arms around me. They are
speechless, and so am I.

20   **The Black Hole**

Weeks later...

"Good morning, Lisa. Hope you had a good night," Terry says, adding that there's coffee made. "Your sister left about twenty minutes ago for her first job interview."

Giving Terry a pat on the back, I ask, "So what'cha doin' on this beautiful Monday morning?"

"Well, I thought I might help you get your work done around here and then maybe you, me and Janie could go to the golf course and knock some balls around."

Thinking that sounds like fun, I agree. "You think Janie will get a ball off the tee this time without tossing her driver into the trash?" We both laugh.

"Anything's possible." Last time we went, Janie ended up throwing her club over the driving range shed, and when everyone started laughing she grabbed a handful of balls and threw them, all of which went further than any ball she'd hit with her club. The Sunday afternoon plaid-clad regulars were practically rolling off the bench with laughter. She stomped off like a child who'd just dropped her ice cream cone on the ground. Of course, the fact that

I was driving balls into the next county wasn't helping her frustration any.

Taking Terry up on her offer to help around the house, I drop in Disco Explosion, turn up the volume and we begin to boogie, hussle and bump our way through the house. With every bed made and the disorderly made orderly again, we move on to the back yard. Deciding that "I Will Survive" should be the next song on the play list, Terry and I set out to conquer the overgrown weeds that are threatening the very life of my flower beds.

Janie, still wearing her best business apparel, suddenly appears in the doorway. "You two are nuts!"

"Hey, sis," I call back, not stopping the beat of the weed eater to the music. "Want to join us?"

"No, thanks. Looks like you two are doing fine all on your own. I'm going to get out of these clothes."

After tackling the back yard, I decide to make an early dinner. Janie doesn't seem to want to talk about her job interview, so I leave it alone and enjoy my dinner. Janie gets a phone call.

"Okay. Meet me there in fifteen minutes," I hear her say.

"Terry, can you take me to the store?"

Speaking up before Terry can answer, I say, "I'll take you, sis."

"I'd rather Terry take me. It may take a while."

"Sure, Janie," Terry says. "Let me grab my keys."

"Hey, I thought we were going to the driving range?"

Hurried and evasive, Janie adds, "I'll be right back. Don't worry."

For some reason, I'm not buying it. Terry comes home without her fifteen minutes later, and my thoughts are confirmed. With Janie being off meth for only two months, I'm really worried about what might be going on. My mind races through all the worst scenarios. I want to know what's going on, and Terry is going to tell me one way or another.

"Where's Janie?" I demand.

"Um…Lisa, I got bad vibes from the guy she drove off with."

Now I'm moving from fearful to furious. It's starting to look like Janie is falling back into the life she's been working so hard to pull herself out of.

"This guy was really rough looking. I tried to convince her not to go, but she insisted that I drop her off. She said she'd call me later for a ride home."

Terry then confesses she and Janie had been driving around looking for jobs and filling out applications a few days earlier. Janie had talked Terry into taking her to a bar off Hwy. 99 for a beer.

"How could you do that, Terry!? Of all the stupid things you could do. You're a recovering alcoholic and addict, and so is she. Coming here, getting clean and learning to do better for herself was her last chance."

"I'm really sorry, Lisa. I think that's where she met him. I was shooting pool and when I turned around she was heading outside with him. She was only gone about fifteen minutes, so I didn't think anything of it."

"That's the problem right there. You didn't think!" Almost screaming, I suddenly realize I'm shaking and my voice is starting to tremble.

"Hey, it's not my fault she can't control herself." Terry's desire for forgiveness is being replaced by an attempt to state the inevitable truth. She hadn't forced Janie into the bar, nor did she put the drink in her hand. But I'm not going to let her off the hook that easily.

"Maybe she's just gone out to get some," Terry yells as she heads for the kitchen.

The list of possible disastrous outcomes continues to grow.

Then Terry makes the one inarguable point, which I already know but don't want to admit. "Lisa, you can't help someone who doesn't want to be helped." That may be true, but I'm going to do my best to make her want to change.

Like a worried mother waiting up for her daughter, I sit on the couch and don't know whether to cry or be angry. I begin to cry. I thought I had made enough of a difference in her life. I thought she was done with deadbeats, drugs, alcohol and lying about her addiction. I thought she was really ready to give herself what she couldn't seem to find anywhere else—a good, clean start.

"Damn it, Terry. I stayed by her side while she shook all night long until she beat meth and alcohol. She did it. She was doing so damn good." I can't hide the anger and disappointment in my voice. "I can't believe she's doing this to herself!"

Terry tells me not to jump to conclusions, but it's too late for that. I grab my cell phone and head for the door. "Let's go, Terry. Take me to the store you dropped her off at, right now."

Trying to convince me not to go, Terry insists that Janie won't be there and that it will be a waste of time, but I make her take me anyway. We sit in the store parking lot for two hours. No Janie. I have Terry take me to the bar where she met the guy, but there's still no sign of her. We sit in the bar parking lot another hour and then go home.

The next morning, I awake to the telephone ringing at 6 a.m., on the other end of the line I hear, "Sis, it's me, Janie," and then tears. I resist the urge to tell her how irresponsible she's been and how much she's made me worry. Instead, I coax her into telling me where she is and if she's all right. Her voice trembling, she tells me she's at the market where Terry dropped her off the day before. I tell her to stay put and that we'll be right there. Terry is up and has already thrown on her clothes. She grabs the keys.

"Oh, my God. There she is." Terry hits the brakes and I'm almost out of the car before it comes to a stop. "What in the world, sis! Are you okay?"

Janie looks like she's been up all night. Her hair is tangled around her dark, sunken eyes and she's trying to hide the bruise on her cheek.

"I tell you what, Lisa. I must be crazy. I am never doing this again, I swear."

She sounds sincere and continues to apologize as I help her into the back seat. Terry throws me the keys and I drive us home. On the way there, I keep looking in the rearview mirror and wonder if this is just a temporary setback. I hope so. She sits with her eyes down and her head turned, still trying to hide the bruise. I can't help but remember when I picked her up from the Portland bus station months ago, her spirit buried under the weight of drugs, sex, anger and hopelessness. My eyes fill with tears, and I have to turn them back to the road.

"I don't want to see you messed up, living on the streets and panhandling again," I say as Janie starts to weep. "You're my little sister, and I only want the best for you." I think, "I hope you want the best for yourself, too, or this isn't going to work." Believing that I see real surrender and acceptance in her eyes, I leave it at that. "I love you, sis. You'll be all right."

"I love you, too."

When we get home, everyone is quiet. Janie goes to her room and closes the door, Terry starts making tea in the kitchen and I can't stop shaking. Sinking into the couch, I close my eyes and take a long, deep breath. The crisis seems to be over, and I realize how emotionally and physically exhausted I am. I feel like I'm sliding into that big, black hole that's been chasing me all of my life. I wonder how much more I can take before I finally fall in.

It's hard enough dealing with what's going on at work. Once again, I'm finding that when I do too good a job and draw too much positive attention, there's always someone who want's to put my head on the chopping block. I've learned that I'm being transferred to a part-time post with a cut in pay and no benefits. I can't help but wonder if it has something to do with a threat I was told about by a couple of ladies who worked in the kitchen at the hospital. I had to turn it in because it was a threat against my life.

The phone rings, and Terry answers it so I don't have to get up. There's an exchange of words but I don't even try to make out what's being said. I'm not home.

"Lisa, your mother is on the phone. She doesn't sound good," Terry says sheepishly as she hands me the phone. She knows that talking to my mom is the last thing I want to do right now.

"Lisa, it's me…" She begins to cry.

"What's wrong, Mom?" Silence. "Mom! Mom!" I can feel a knot in my stomach tightening and I wonder if this will ever stop.

"I'm here, Lisa. I just hate calling you because I know

you're going through a lot with Janie there, but you are the only one I can call. You're the only one who understands."

I know what's coming next. The same thing that always comes next when the conversation starts out like this.

"Your Dad left us again. He took the RV and said he was going to run it through the wash and be right back. That was yesterday. When he didn't come home, I checked my purse. He took every penny we had." Her voice cracks, and I can tell she's about to lose it.

"Mom, he's been doing this to you since the day you met him. What don't you get? I love you, but you need to put yourself first for once. I would think that by now you would have learned that every time he meets some floozy he's gone!"

"I know, I know. You're right, but why does he continue to do this to me?" When she says that it's obvious she still doesn't get it, or rather, she still doesn't want to get it.

"Mom! Stop feeling sorry for yourself! You're stronger than that." I'm trying not to let out the stream of frustration and resentment that has been building over the last forty years. But after last night, and all I've had to go through with Janie, this time I want her to really hear me.

"Our family never had anything because we moved all the time, and I used to blame him for every time we had to move and I got beat up at a new school. I blamed him for every time we came home from school and our toys were sold, the dog had been given away and we were loaded into the car without so much as a moment's notice." I suddenly realize I've never really told her exactly how I feel. "I don't blame him anymore, Mom. I blame you, because you could have stopped it all."

The phone goes dead.

I sit and fume for a few minutes and then call her back. "Why did you hang up on me? I love you, but it's time I tell it like it is. Don't you know what kind of hell us kids went through? All you had to do was walk away. You allowed him to keep doing this to you—and—us, over and over again, and every time, he knew you'd take him back."

"I know, I know. I am so sorry," she says, crying.

Just then, Janie races out of her bedroom and throws up before she gets to the bathroom, all over my new carpet.

"Terry, please help Janie. She's in the bathroom."

"What's wrong with Janie?" Mom yells over the phone.

"Nothing. She just has a bad cold or something. She's been off meth now for over two months and she's doing really well…and getting better every day." I swallow hard on that one, but it wouldn't do any good to tell her the truth.

Mom goes right back to wondering what she's going to do, and I keep listening with an occasional "Yeah, Mom" thrown in. The list of Dad's faults, betrayals and abuses goes on endlessly until I just can't stand it. I've had to deal with this my entire life.

"Mom, when are you going to stop this? I want you to really listen to me. Every time Dad leaves, you call me and drive me nuts! What do you want from me?" She doesn't have an answer. "In a few weeks, he'll come back when the money's gone and you'll take him back like you always do. Haven't you figured out yet that you allow this to happen? People will treat you exactly the way you allow them to."

All I hear is muffled crying on the other end. I hope she's starting to understand.

"You are beautiful, Mom. He doesn't leave because of something you're doing or not doing. Stop belittling your-self like this. I think you should get some help. Go talk to someone so that when he does come back you can slam the door in his face and tell him to get lost. That's what you need to do!"

"I know, I know. But I can't. I love him!" Her crying becomes a sobbing breakdown. Totally exhausted, I fall back onto the couch and let her voice fade away for a moment as I ask myself again if this will ever stop. Do I need to apply to my own life what I am preaching to her? Across the room, Terry struggles to get Janie back into her room as Janie slams the door in her face.

"Lisa, she's made a mess," Terry yells. "Do you want me to clean it up?"

"No. I'll do it in a minute."

Mom's voice on the other end of the line catches my attention again. "Lisa? Lisa!? I'm not feeling well, so I'm going to go lie down. I love you. Can I call you if I need to?"

"Sure, Mom. You can call me anytime, day or night, even if it's 2 a.m." Pausing for a moment, I add, "Please, for all of our sakes, don't do anything stupid. I love you, and I'm only telling you what you've taught me. Take your own advice."

"I know, sweetheart. I love you, Lisa. Good night."

"Good night, Mom."

Terry comes out of the bathroom with the cleaning bucket and I thank her for helping Janie. As I go to the kitchen sink and start filling the bucket with hot water, I try not to look at Terry because tears are swelling up in my eyes. Terry grabs me, and I begin to sob and shake in her arms. I don't know how much more of this I can take. Then I feel the anger coming on.

21 — Bread and Wine

"When is all of this going to stop!?" I yell. "What am I suppose to do, Terry? The two of you aren't helping out. I finally get rid of the drug-addict roommates, but then you came along and started drinking…Janie ends up here to get off meth…I have a crazy guy threatening my life at work…and now I'm about to lose my home!"

Terry opens a soda and hands it to me. I think she's worried about which direction my anger will take. I know I'm scaring her so I take the drink, soften my tone and try to calm down. "Thanks, Terry. I know this isn't your fault, I'm just really angry about my life right now. If this is the way my life was supposed to turn out, maybe I would have been better off not being born, just like my grandpa said."

"But Lisa, maybe you were born to do exactly what you've been doing your entire life: helping others. Don't you remember what the blue angel told you? God taught you to be strong because he knew you were going to need to be, not just for yourself, but for us, too. I don't know if me or Janie would have made it this far without you."

I throw the soda across the room, and as it hits the

wall I yell, "I don't want to be strong right now. I just want some peace and quiet!" As I sit down on the couch, a sinking, sick feeling creeps into my stomach. My nerves are fried. For almost three hours, I sit and silently cry while Terry stays by my side to make sure I'm all right.

I cry when I think about what others have done to me—robbed me, raped me, tried to murder me, stole from me, left me without, hit me, lied about me, set me up and hated me for no other reason than their own self-righteous prejudice. It is my time to be angry, and I have every right to be.

Getting up off the couch, I walk down the hall to my room, open the door and begin to throw things off the bed. I break every picture on the wall, rip all the clothes in my closet in half and flip my bed upside down. I knock holes in the walls with my fists, break everything I can get my hands on and then collapse on top of the mountain of debris that is my life. All my possessions are broken into a million pieces, just like my heart.

Completely exhausted, I lay motionless. Then raising my head, I look around the room to see what I've done. I feel nothing. Knowing I can't just stay there, I push myself up from the broken glass and notice Terry sitting on the end of the mattress. I didn't even know she was there. It must have been like sitting in the middle of a hurricane.

"Lisa? Lisa, you're bleeding! Here, let me help you." I look down and realize I have cuts all over my hands and arms. Blood is running down my arms and dripping onto the carpet.

"It doesn't hurt, Terry. Really, it doesn't hurt anymore." I tell her calmly.

"Looks like this has been coming on for a long time,"

She says, trying to humor me.

"Yeah, looks like it."

Terry says she's going to fix me a place on the couch for the night and that she'll clean up my room tomorrow. I tell her not to bother since I'm going to lose the house anyway. She guides me into the bathroom, helps me wash the blood off my arms and makes me a bed on the couch. Terry hands me a couple of pain killers and a glass of water then places a cool washcloth on my forehead and turns out the light.

"Good night, Lisa."

Everything seems so quiet now, and I wonder how Janie managed to sleep through the commotion. I guess she has her own demons to battle tonight. I close my eyes and try to pray, but even my prayers are getting short these days. I fall asleep without finishing.

The next morning, I wake up to the vacuum humming and Terry telling Janie what happened the night before. It's hard to hear the account from the outside looking in. Sleep gave me some peace, but now I'm remembering what caused last night, and I know nothing has magically changed overnight. I begin to cry again and end up spending the rest of the day on the couch. Terry and Janie leave for a while and return several hours later with groceries.

"Hi, sis," Janie says as she leans over and kisses my forehead. "How are you feeling?"

"Like shit. I don't feel good at all."

"I'm sorry for what I did. I won't do it again." I can tell she's feeling a little guilty for possibly contributing to my mental state.

"It's not your fault, Janie. A lot has happened this year, and with Mom calling yesterday, well…I guess I went a little over the top."

Janie adds, "Well it's about time! All your life you never took revenge, you never hurt anybody and you always did the right thing. How does it feel to be normal like the rest of us?"

Other people may have called me "goody goody," but I've always known I'm as flawed as the next person. I've just never shown it to this extent before. "It felt pretty damn good! But I broke all my things."

Terry comes in with a large picture of a ship lost at sea in a storm. Handing it to me, she says a friend gave it to her but she wants me to have it instead. I try to object, but she insists. I thank her for such a wonderful present. And so appropriate.

"Here. I made this for you. Don't ever lose it." Janie hands me a small beaded purse with a crystal tucked down in the center. "It took me a long time to make that." Ever the ageless flower child, she can always make me smile.

"Thanks guys. These are wonderful." They both huddle around me in a group hug as I begin to shake and cry. Lately, every time I start to cry, I shake inside. Each time, it's harder to stop.

"I'm sorry, but I'm really tired. Can I just sleep a little more?"

"You sleep. When you wake up, Terry and I will have dinner ready, okay?"

"Sounds good," I answer. In reality, I am getting sick to the point that I no longer care. All I want to do is sleep in the hopes that when I wake up, I will feel better. Every time I have felt like this in the past, I've always gotten back up, brushed myself off and moved on. But this time, the depression is too deep. For the first time in my life, I don't have plans B and C, much less a plan A. The black hole is closing in.

I wake up a few hours later, trying to remember what I just dreamed…it is very important. Closing my eyes I can see myself in a peaceful place where I know I'm safe and everything is going to be all right. Then I know what it is I have to do: I will fast and pray. I ask Janie and Terry to come sit with me.

"I want to let the two of you know what I've decided to do about my situation," I say. Janie begins to cry and asks if I'm going to do something stupid. "No. You don't have to worry. I've already done enough of that," I say trying to reassure them. "I'm going into my room to fast and pray, and I'm not coming out until I have the answers."

"How long will that be?" Terry asks in a worried tone.

"I don't know…hours, days, weeks, months, even years…if that's what it takes."

"Lisa, I am really worried about you," Janie says.

"I'm worried about me, too. That's why I need to do this."

They ask what they can do to help, and I tell them to take care of the house, keep things quiet and leave me to myself. "No knocking on the door, no phone calls. Don't interrupt me unless there's an emergency or someone's dead. Okay?"

They both agree they can do that, and I ask if they can go to the store for me. Reaching for a pen, I write down what I want: four bottles of red wine, four loaves of baguette bread, a white robe and three of the largest white candles they can find. Getting the money box down from the top of my closet, I take out $200 that I've put away to buy a piano keyboard. I give it to Terry and tell her to keep $50, give $50 to Janie and use the rest for what I need.

"Now I need to sleep. I love you guys. Don't worry. I think this will help me see things more clearly." Lying back down on the couch, I tell Janie to put the things I've asked for in my room so that when I wake up I can go in and close the door behind me.

"Lisa, why wine, bread and candles?" Janie asks.

"I'm going to take communion every night at 7 p.m. The white candles represent the father, the son and the holy spirit, which I'm calling on to help me."

They shut the door behind them as they leave.

I wake up to Terry coming through the door with two bags of groceries in her arms. "I'll put these in your room, Lisa." Getting up, I follow her into my bedroom and check the bags to make sure I have everything I'll need.

Janie comes in, wraps her arms around me and whispers, "I love you, sis. If it weren't for you, I wouldn't be here right now." Smiling, I take her hand and squeeze it. She knows. Hesitantly, they leave me alone, and I set about getting ready for a journey that is both frightening and a relief. I set the three candles on top of the dresser with one bottle of wine and one loaf of bread, while the rest go into my closet for later. I have a bathroom connected to my room, and I hang my new white robe on the door's hook and place a note pad and pen next to the candles. "Today is going to be a very long day," I think to myself as I set the alarm for 6:30 p.m. and climb into bed.

Day one: I wake up to the alarm and look at the clock. It's 6:30 in the evening, and I get up and take a shower. Afterward, I light the candles one-by-one and say a prayer for strength, understanding and most of all, the courage to keep going. I pour an inch of wine in the bottom of a glass, break off a small piece of bread and place it on a saucer.

Saying a prayer, I eat the bread, sip the wine and reset the clock for seven o'clock in the morning. It is time to pray and open my spirit to God's direction. Down on my knees, I pray all through the night and into the morning. When the alarm goes off at 7 a.m. I reset it again for 6:30 p.m. and go to sleep. I will pray for twelve hours and sleep for twelve hours until I know what to do.

Day two: the depression makes it hard to concentrate for twelve hours at a time, so sleeping and praying take on an uneven rhythm, with sleep being in the majority. I no longer have a sense of time, and the hours simply flow one into the other.

Day three: much the same. A lot of thinking, praying and crying—not necessarily in that order. I remain determined to keep the ritual going until I have a clear mind and the answers I need.

Day four: I awake exhausted with a weariness I've never experienced. Even the effort of getting on my knees to pray seems too much for my body to withstand. My mind lacks the strength to command my body to do its will.

It is becoming difficult to carry out my plan as I intended. I worry that I may not receive my answer, and this is making me angry and afraid. Memories are surfacing and muddling my thoughts, and I feel as though I'm stuck between the present and the past. All I do is cry and shake. Without the strength to kneel and pray, I climb back into bed and pull the covers over my head. It seems the black hole is closing in.

I awake again and decide that taking a shower might make me feel better and enable me to carry on. Standing under the warm stream, I let the ribbons of water flow over my head and face hoping it will wash away the pain.

The next thing I realize, I'm lying on the bottom of the tub, the shower pouring ice cold water over me. I jump up and turn the water off, not knowing how long I've been there. Looking in the mirror, I see that my lips are blue and my skin is red and tinted with patches of blue. As I stare at myself in the mirror I begin to cry and wonder who I am. The longer I stare the angrier I become, remembering all those who hurt me in my lifetime.

I grab the scissors and begin cutting off my hair. I cut and cut until there is nothing left, and for a brief moment my spirit and body was torn. I look down at my hair lying on the floor and begin to cry even harder. I reach down to the bottom of my soul and call upon God to help me and show me what to do. Having offered my most desperate plea, I manage to make my way back to bed where I fell asleep and begin to dream.

Day five: when I awoke, everything felt different. The sun is shining on my face through the window. I feel peaceful and all my worries seem so small. I know that today is the day my fasting and praying will end. It is over. I know exactly what I need to do.

Going into the bathroom I stand in front of the mirror and decide to shave the rest of my hair off as a marker of my new beginning. I feel happy, reassured, safe, awakened and blessed, but most of all, the answers are within me and God has once again lifted me and given me new hope. I take a shower, get dressed and make my bed. Once everything is straightened up in my room, I light the candles one last time, take a deep breath and stand in front of my bedroom door.

I slowly open the door and stand in the threshold wondering. If I leave this room and return to my day-to-day life, will I be safe? What will happen when I cross that line and have to face the other side? I'm also worried about what Terry and Janie's reactions will be when they see what I have done to myself. As I look up, I see Terry standing in the hallway.

"Oh, my God! Lisa. Oh, sweetie." She is in shock as she stands and stares at me. Janie opens her bedroom door, sees me and stops. Neither of them rush to hug me or ask questions. They just stand there, staring at me as I wipe tears from my face and try to look as brave as I can.

"What's wrong?" I ask hesitantly.

"It's just that you seem so…sacred and look so…different. Is it okay to hug you?" Terry asks.

I nod, and Terry wraps her arms around me. Janie joins in.

"I can't believe you cut off all your hair! You look great," Terry says as she runs her hand along the side of my head.

"What happened?" Janie asks.

"Well, sis, it's a long story. All I know is that I got my answer and I know what I'm going to do. But can I get a hot cup of tea first?" My smile reassures them that everything is going to be all right.

Terry dashes to the kitchen. "I'll make your favorite—Jasmine green tea!"

"Thanks, Terry. I love you, woman."

Janie holds my hand all the way to the living room. While we wait on the couch for the tea, she sits with her head on my shoulder. We're both quiet until Terry returns from the kitchen.

"You look very rested, and you really look great bald," Terry comments.

"Do I really?" I run my hand over the top of my head.

"Well, I may just keep it this way then."

The two of them ask me questions about what happened over the last five days and I answer as best I can until I'm so tired I fall asleep on the couch. Getting up a few hours later, I see Janie asleep in my bed. It's nice to see her so peaceful. I find a pen and paper, sit back down on the couch and start listing everything I'm going to do. First, I'm going to put my home up for sale. Second, I'm going to send Janie back to my sister's house in Missouri. Third, I'm going to get a new job, move into my own place and help Terry get a place of her own. It all seems so simple.

§

I listed my home with an agent, and it sold the next day. I found a new job as a maintenance technician, sent Janie to my sister's house, got Terry into her own place and moved myself into a new apartment. How peaceful is that! I love my new tranquil, organized and clean space. For once, I only have myself to take care of, and I'm feeling better every day. Even when I have a bad day, I only have *my own* bad day to deal with—and not everyone else's. That makes my life a lot easier, and it's also easier to get back up when I fall down.

God's lessons of forgiveness, and turning my anger and pain over to him, saved my life, my spirit and my sanity.

I still live what I call a strange yet remarkable life.

The End

...or only the beginning?

We can not force others to change,

but we can become a positive influence

and mentor to those who *Seek*

For those who represent *Hope*

represent *Love*

Through Love, we will each find

our *Peace*

Lisa L. Everly

The Quiet Snow

A poem by Mary Everly

Thinking of you!

I think of you today, as I behold
soft, white flakes of snow falling
gently down on my outer window sill,
so careful to not disturb the cold,
sleeping earth below. I trace your
name along the frosted glass with my
index finger, still numb from winter's chill.
In a trance like state of awe, I stop and
press my face into a wonderland of white.
The beauty of it all overwhelms my very soul.
No two the same. A unique design of the
master's hand. A peaceful, almost ghostly
shiver runs up my spine. Like the quiet
snow, we too are his creation, made in his
image, yet one. I laugh to myself with
humble respect, as I behold his greatness.
I can see him in all things, I see him in your
face. As I think of you today, and wait the
endless, no two the same that grows.
I wait now to consider, the dawning of the rose.

I love you, Lisa.
Love, Mom
June 14, 2005

The Dawning of the Rose

I lie in silent obscurity beneath the cool,
moist earth awaiting spring.
I am cold, withered, thirsty, and alone.
Longing so to live again.
I pray, how long O'Lord shall I rest here,
your stay hand upon me? Holding back
time for just the right day. I am so fragile,
and humble, in this ground, destined to be
my bed from the beginning.
A masterful plan, designed on my behalf.
So, I shall sleep for now, and wait for the
day of your glory to appear. What's this I see?
A ray of hope shines through, with the faint
flicker from the sun's light upon my face.
Filling my body with warmth and energy,
I rise upward. How grand to stretch out
again. Bursting forth as a new born babe,
I cry out with joy, I hold my head high,
and press onward. At last, I am. My velvet
petals unfold, drenched with dew. Like
teardrops from heaven they fall, as they
dry in the morning sun, I am crowned
with a kaleidoscope of radiant colors'
never before seen. The breeze
whispers, and I am kissed by angels
with the sweetest fragrance ever known.
I stand tall, in all my splendor, and the
earth knows, the miracle God gave
to the world, in the dawning of the rose.

I love you, Lisa.
Love, Mom.

A   My Brother's Keeper

I want to share with you one of the experiences I had while meditating up in the California desert. I don't meditate as often as I'd like, but I'm working on that because it brings such peace to my soul.

As a child I taught myself to meditate, probably as a means to let my mind escape what was going on in my physical surroundings. As an adult, it's my light that connects me with God, and it clears my mind.

I climbed to the top of a rocky hill about six miles outside of Victorville. It was about two hours before sunset. The wind was warm yet refreshing, and the sky was filled with huge clouds that glided through the sky like giant balls of cotton candy. The pastel blues and pinks swirled onto white, which danced through the canvas of my mind as the wind swept through my hair. I took a deep breath, raised my hands to the sky and yelled "Thank you, God! For everything!" I closed my eyes and stood in such thankfulness and peace as the sun bathed my face. How warm it was and how special I felt to be alive.

Just then, I heard a little voice coming from behind

me. I quickly turned around and was face-to-face with a man who looked like he'd just crawled out from under the rock I was standing on.

"You're a little charismatic, aren't you?" he said with a sarcastic tone, and then in a friendlier voice, "Don't worry. I'm harmless. God as my witness," he said, raising his hand to the sky.

"Okay, the rocks as my witness." Then he began to laugh.

"I didn't see anyone up here, so I thought this would be a good place to pray and meditate," I replied.

"Oh sure, I got no problem with that. But before you go into your little 'God loves me' routine, can you spare an old fart some change?" he said, picking at the sores on his arm.

"First, answer me this: what 'God loves me' routine are you talking about?"

"Oh, hell. You know, the one where you ask me to pray with you and ask Jesus into my heart." He was getting annoyed at having to explain the seemingly obvious, process that was delaying me from giving him my change. "You know. THAT stuff!"

"Well, why don't you explain it to me since you know what you're talking about."

"Don't you play dumb with me. You know what I'm talking about! You'll tell me a story and then trick me into praying with you, hoping you can turn me into one of those 'evil Christians,'" he laughed even harder as he clicked his thumbs together with his forefingers and raised them to the sky.

I couldn't help it. I had to laugh, too. "Oh, you mean those people who are best at judging others?"

"Yeah, them!" he said excitedly.

"…and those who really wouldn't care if you died right now, much less where you'd go after that?" I continued.

"Yeah!"

"Ah ha!" I jumped back and laughed.

"Hey! You're pretty sneaky," he said as he began to trip over a small rock when I caught his fall.

Trying to calm things down a bit before someone ended up falling over the side, I said, "Why don't you sit down here for a minute and get some rest?"

I kept my eye on the guy as I went back to my truck. When I returned with a couple bottles of water and a bag of chips, he changed his attitude from the disrespect he'd displayed earlier.

"I didn't come up here to interfere with your life. I only came to pray and meditate because it's quiet and beautiful. What did you come up here for?"

"Oh, the same as you," he mumbled through a mouthful of BBQ chips. "I come up here all the time. It's as close to God as I'll ever get."

As he drank down the last sip from the first bottle, I opened the other and handed it to him.

"Why, thank you," he said politely. And then letting out a long belch he added, "You were lucky to find this place."

I knew then that I wasn't going to get back to my serene, pastel canvas unless I somehow incorporated him into my bliss.

"Well, Mr. Rock Man, I am going over there to pray and meditate. If you care to join me, there will be a dinner of your choice afterward. Anything you want, on me." I got up, brushed the dust off my pants, walked over to the edge and sat down. I heard the potato chip package crinkle behind me.

Not opening my eyes, I told him, "There's a trash bag in the back of my truck. You can put it in there if you want."

"Okay," he yelled as he hurried to my truck.

As I took a long, deep breath, I asked God to help my new friend, adding that he was just down on his luck and needed a new outlook. I figured the prayer was being answered when the guy sat down four feet from me and tried to coax his legs into the lotus position. Getting as close to cross-legged as he could, he raised his hands and let out a startling "Ohmmm…Awweee!" Then in the loudest tent revival voice he could muster, he yelled out, "Help me, God! For I know I am a sinner!"

With my requirement seemingly fulfilled, he added, "Now can I please have dinner?" He began laughing himself into a crazed frenzy, and I thought he was going to rock himself right off the edge of the cliff.

"Hey! You'd better watch what you're doing or you're going to…"

I didn't get to finish my warning because just then, he stood up, got his legs tangled and fell over the edge. He must have rolled downhill fifteen to twenty feet before catching himself on a rock large enough to hold his body weight.

"Hey, are you okay?" I yelled down to him. "Don't move or you'll be road kill, for sure."

"Don't make me laugh any harder or I'm going to die—for sure," he said calmly, with a very concerned and focused tone.

"Hang on. I'll help you. Don't move."

I didn't know what to do, but I hoped I could find a

solution. I looked around. There was a long, broken tree branch a few feet away, and although it was a long shot, I thought it might be our only chance. I crawled down as far as I could without putting myself in danger and held out the branch. It just barely reached him.

"That thing won't hold me!" he yelled.

"You believe in God, don't you?"

"Oh, hell," he yelled again. "Yes, yes. Yes, I do!"

"Then ask him to help you," I told him.

"God, please help me. I'm sorry! I don't want to die."

I moved closer. He grabbed the end with one hand, and I pulled as hard as I could. Gravel began to rain down the rocky mountainside, and I could hear his voice crack as he pleaded for help. We were in one heck of a situation.

"God, give me strength!" I prayed.

With my left hand, I grabbed hold of a rock with all my might. With my right, I pulled him up a few inches at a time until he could grab the branch with both hands. Then, easing myself up a little at a time, I took him with me until he was clear of the edge and could help himself.

"For a girl, you're pretty strong. How did you do that?"

Once the panic had subsided the anger set in, and I told him just what I thought about the situation. "It's people like you who put people like me in situations like this," I yelled, "because of your disregard toward life, God and most of all yourself! If you're going to throw your life away, then do it, but don't try to take other people with you." I was very upset, to say the least. On top of everything else, the water was gone.

I threw the tree branch as far as I could and bent down to catch my breath. That's when I heard him begin to cry out loud. I turned around and saw that man on his knees, wailing. "Oh, my God. Oh, my God. What have I done? Please help me!"

He touched my heart this time, and I knew he was serious. I went over and sat down next to him, put my arm over his shoulder and began to pray with him. Afterwards, I helped him to his feet and, as dirty as he was, I gave him a big hug. He apologized to me for what had happened and the way he'd behaved. I looked down and watched a scorpion crawl under a rock.

"What's your name?" I asked.

"Jim."

"Well Jim, if I take you to a station will you clean yourself up so we can go to dinner? Your choice."

He began to cry again. "You mean you're still buying me dinner?"

"Of course. I always keep my word," I said, smiling at him.

We got in the truck and drove down the hill to the gas station, where Jim washed up and tried to make himself presentable. He chose the Steer 'n Stein for dinner. As I sat having dinner with someone I didn't know yet felt compassion for, I realized that his attempt to ruin my day actually brightened my pastel sky.

That evening, Jim told me the story of how he had run off on his wife and kids one night with another woman. When the excitement of that had wore off, he was left an alcoholic who ended up homeless and panhandling. He wiped tears from his eyes when he said, "I got lost, and now my life is catching up with me I guess."

I asked him if he had any family. He said he did, back in Texas where he was born. "I have two brothers and I think my..." he began to cry again, "mother, if she's still alive."

"It's okay," I said. "You know what you have to do. When you get there, tell your family that God brought you back to your senses. Then get a job, start over and keep your head up because God has your back!"

Later that evening, I took Jim to the Greyhound station and bought him a one-way ticket home. As I watched him climb up the stairs and hand his ticket to the driver, I knew he'd do what was right. He'd find his way back home and pick up where he left off.

I believe it's not the plans we have, but rather the plans God has for us. My spiritual journey has been quite an experience, and I'm sure yours has been and will be, too. One never knows the road another must travel, but we can still count on each other and reach out to those soul's longing to find their way back home.

Phrixus

Cephas

B — Thoughts About God

When I was very young...

I went to my mother and asked, "Who is God?" She talked to me about her thoughts but also encouraged me to find out for myself.

I began to understand that God created the heavens and the Earth, and God created me. I learned to be alone, clear my mind and concentrate on connecting with Spirit through meditation. I asked questions and listened carefully for God's answer. Sometimes the answer would come as insight, sometimes through an observation and sometimes in my dreams.

I began to see God in the beautiful things he created, like delicate flowers, picturesque skies, beautiful valleys and majestic trees. People and the ways we help each other are also manifestations of God. He revealed himself through the angels he sent to me, as well as through earthly angels who helped when called upon. God is everywhere. While he may seem unreachable, he is always near.

I discovered that God is kind, loving, peaceful and passionate at his work. He knows justice and the hearts of all people. I learned that I'm made in his likeness and that no matter what humankind may try to change, God's love far surpasses man's dictates.

The key to spiritual success

All spiritual journeys follow a different path. We are each unique, learn in our own ways and make different choices. What is similar is that we are all searching for the same thing—a deeper understanding of and closer relationship with God.

God offers everyone the opportunity to walk in the light. It is not reserved for just a few, but rather for all who believe. This doesn't mean we have to be perfect; it just means we will be forgiven.

One of the greatest lessons I've learned on my journey is forgiveness. It is the *key to spiritual success*. Practicing forgiveness allows me to let go of negativity and cleanse my spirit, enabling me to remain open to the positive possibilities God wants to share with me. I could have easily chosen to hurt others as much as I had been hurt, but what would I have gained? I would have ended up in prison or dead, my soul lost to the same evil that came against me. Revenge and retaliation will only destroy us in the end.

When we say to God, "I forgive those who have hurt me. It is not for me to be their judge, so I put justice in your hands. Only you truly know their hearts," we are choosing to walk in the light and save ourselves from the second hand of evil that didn't get us the first time. It is only through complete faith in God that we can walk away with an open heart and move forward on our journey.

Where was God when I needed him?

God should not be blamed for the negative things that happen in this world. The Adversary—evil—has but a short time and will do his best to hurt humankind and cause as many as possible to fall from grace. Evil often appears as good and will tempt many people. There are also those who are caught in the crossfire of the spiritual war between good and evil that's been waging since the beginning of time.

Don't think that God isn't there for you when something terrible happens. He is. You may see him in the firefighter who rescues you or the neighbor who takes you in. If you open your heart and understand God, you will find him everywhere. I know there is a time and place for everything in his will. To God, nothing is impossible. Therefore, I understand that I must trust what God shows me. Only he knows how all the pieces fit together, so when things don't seem to make sense, I remember that I'm only looking at a few pieces of the puzzle.

I don't question God's work but give praise for the lessons he's providing. Through lessons we receive his blessings, and through blessings we receive spiritual gifts. Sometimes it's hard to understand the purpose of a lesson. But in the end, I believe the results explain everything.

We have eyes and do not see

Sometimes, we refuse to recognize things we can not physically see. With a believing heart, however, we can spiritually see what may teach us more about this world, the universe, humankind and the spiritual realm. Humankind is allowing itself to become blind and is slowly destroying its abilities, which is one of the reasons even geniuses can only reach the capacity of using 10 to 12 percent of their minds. The other percentage of our intelligence is exercised spiritually, and that can only be done with God's help.

What God has made, no man shall tear apart

Today I am not only living, I am a living witness that God loves me and will never leave me. Once, I began to fall away from the God I'd known all my life because of what people said. Others loved me until they found out I was a lesbian and then they began to say God hated me because I was a lesbian and that I was going to hell. I know now not to listen to such people, because they only lead others away from God.

I want to tell my brothers and sisters, that God loves them very much. God knows our hearts and therefore knows our pain. Seek out your own journey and let God be the light. The obstacles in your path are only there to stop you from finding the love God has for you. Pray to God, and he will help you to walk right over them. Keep your head up—God has your back.

I see this world as a beautiful place where we can live, grow, share, learn and love while teaching each other to become the best we can possibly be. I also realize that task is more difficult than it has ever been before. The world is a testing ground. I believe our spiritual future is determined by what we do here and how we treat others, regardless of how we are treated. I love the Mahatma Gandhi quote: "Be the change you want to see in the world," because we are all indeed pieces of the puzzle. Each one of us must be spiritually complete to make it whole again. Learning to live together peacefully in this diverse world is one of the most important steps. How can we quietly go within ourselves to find our connection with God if we are constantly fighting among ourselves?

Take care, my friend. Should our paths ever cross, may we share the same kindness through love and peace in our hearts as God has for us.

CPSIA information can be obtained
at www.ICGtesting.com
Printed in the USA
BVHW031715180620
581648BV00002B/77/J

9 781434 378774